Lincoln's Missing Papers and Chair

By
Edmond Ankony
Richard Ankony

Dedication

To my father, a kind, honest and selfless man whom I have loved dearly throughout my entire life.

I was blessed to have you as my father.

God sent me into good hands and I have been forever thankful and grateful to call you, Dad.

Though time and space may someday separate us, we will meet again at the sure and certain Resurrection to the life of the world to come, to rejoice with Mom who awaits us with our ancestors, at the banquet, in the Great Hall of our people.

In honor and respect of my father, Edmond Frank Ankony, this book could not have been written without his lifelong stories that he told to me throughout my life.

Introduction

This book started out with the most innocent of intentions until it acquired a life of it's own which left me with the impression that it had become something out of the movie, <u>National Treasure</u>.

My 98-year-old father of whom I love dearly is my oldest friend on the earth has requested that I be his courier for this book.

Throughout the years my father has told me many stories in detail of yesteryear and one story in particular stood out since about 1990.

That story of which this book is about was an event my father witnessed around 1932 at Independence Hall, Philadelphia, Pennsylvania.

My father witnessed certain pieces of fabric upholstery being torn and taken from the original Abraham Lincoln's chair in which he was assassinated in on April 14, 1865.

My father further read at that time certain original Abraham Lincoln papers that were also there <u>that were taken</u>, of which the contents that were described to me I found to be disturbing.

The problem is, the original Abraham Lincoln's assassination chair is believed for the last 85 years since 1929 to be at the Henry Ford Museum, Dearborn, Michigan.

It is stated that Henry Ford, the automobile magnate, bought the original chair in 1929 and brought it up to Henry Ford Museum, Dearborn, Michigan to be put on display and <u>kept there ever since</u>.

Yet my 98-year-old father told me over and over again that he and his friends had seen and made contact with the original Abraham Lincoln chair in 1932 at Independence Hall, Philadelphia, Pennsylvania.

Upon my investigation, I was told from someone in the know, that the records at Independence Hall at that time, "<u>of those that survived</u>" were "<u>spotty at best</u>."

So on one side of the equation stands Henry Ford's empire with all its resources and influential expert historians making claim that their chair is original while on the other side stands just my 98 year old father and myself who disagree.

To begin with, I am not an historian and I say upfront that I can't compete with them nor is it my intentions to discredit them or anyone in any way.

What I am is a state licensed private investigator/private eye and a state licensed polygraph interrogator/examiner along with being a retired 25-year lawman.

This is what I am and all that I make claim too.

With this in mind I could not help but wonder that on one hand an automotive giant, Henry Ford, has claimed with 100% certainty since 1929, that the chair, which Abraham Lincoln was assassinated in, is in his possession and is the original assassination chair.

By claiming such has allowed Henry Ford to draw millions of people to his museum to pay $20 to $45 dollars a head, at present prices, to look upon and gaze at this perceived original antique with star struck eyes.

Yet my father on the other hand I know as an honest man both sane and with clear mind has never lied to me and has nothing to gain by stating, "The original chair cannot be at two places at the same time, Richard. It cannot be at Independence Hall around 1932 and at the Henry Ford Museum-Greenfield Village since 1929!"

With this statement, my investigative journey began.

R9CFF

All my life I have been a hunter for the truth, which has led me into the polygraph profession.

As a polygraph examiner for the last 35 years I would have to sort out deception from the truth and then test against that deception and truth to reach a diagnostic evaluation.

As a private investigator I gather facts of a case of which I am investigating to bring closure to the matter. Many times I had to gather fragmented pieces and place them together to create a composite or picture as if a jigsaw puzzle to determine or reconstruct as best as I can what transpired.

As a police officer, as with all police officers, I had to study and observe suspicious characteristics or abnormal behavioral traits of people's behavior that are outside the norm of every day life.

For honest people usually act within certain known norms while deviants with their criminal mind usually act in a totally different fashion. The wolf in sheep clothing is the best analogy of the criminal mind for they are opportunists and predators that prey upon the unsuspecting and the innocent with their secret schemes and webs of deceit.

Despite this background by no means is my observation and technique perfect yet it has withstood the test of time and has led me to certain truths.

In the same way I know "out there" there are historians hunting for critical facts which would lead them to establish certain truths of the past with just fragmented investigative leads that reflect on matters of state and the human species.

When I first started to do this book it was my only intention to take my father's information, which I found to be in my opinion, "very important."

Then take this information and present these facts eventually to worthy historians of the Civil War Period. This in turn would help them to focus their search of this material, if they were looking for it, from say seven billion people down to a mere hundred or so.

So hopefully, this book was not done in vain for I still believe that the truth is "out there" regarding Abraham Lincoln's assassination chair and the contents of these original papers that have gone missing will ultimately be discovered by a professional historian with resolve, perseverance and persistent search techniques that will bring closure to this matter.

That was my intention in the beginning of this matter, which was to help future Civil War historians with clues and also to raise my father's spirits so that he felt he was still an integral part of society by contributing to society certain truths.

Yet as the facts were uncovered regarding the chair and papers and after going over my father's details, this book metamorphosized and took on a life of it's own.

All I did was just follow the facts whether fragmented or complete to where it led me and that was the Abraham Lincoln's assassination chair claimed to be held at the Henry Ford Museum with 100% certainty appears to be either deliberately or inadvertently misleading.

Therefore all I am doing is telling you another side of the story from my father's perspective about Abraham Lincoln's assassination chair, which appears to be totally contrary to what the public is being told by Henry Ford, or the Henry Ford Museum (Greenfield Village Museum).

In addition, I will further discuss original critical papers that my father was witness too that belonged to Abraham Lincoln which was read and taken and present to you what happened to these critical papers and who was last to be seen with them.

These papers, in my opinion, of what my father claims is quite different from what I was told or led to believe about Abraham Lincoln.

Though I am certain the historians know more of Abraham Lincoln and the Civil War then I do, I will therefore accept their professional opinion of their interpretive significance of these papers in question in advance.

Yet despite that, I know firsthand in certain matters of state, that "We the People" are being deliberately misled to believe in many matters that is not the truth but rather being misled through deceit and treachery which is designed to serve a self-serving agenda of certain men and women's rein of power in high places.

So remember this book is not just about "The Chair" or "The Papers" but rather it is also a journey into the possible realm of <u>deliberate</u> deception to extract from the innocent their monetary resources and mislead them by setting up a false front of originality to serve one's self-serving agenda.

So whatever outcome this book will take, I must shortly thereafter depart from this sanitized version of "The Chair" being told to the American people since 1929 and return back to my real world of the devastated falsely accused and the "perfectly possessed" deceptive criminal savages.

That said, my father's story begins sometime around 1932 and according to my 98-year-old father, Edmond Ankony, he and his friends entered Independence Hall, Philadelphia, Pennsylvania to look at the exhibits on display.

While visiting this museum they came across the Liberty Bell and studied it's history while touching the bell and it's famous crack.

While they were there and according to my father many of the items on display could be physically touched and handled without the presence of security to prevent it.

As they were enjoying the exhibits they came across the original Lincoln's chair (rocking chair) that Abraham Lincoln was sitting on when he was shot at the Ford Theater on Good Friday, April 14, 1865.

The exhibits had placards next to them stating that <u>they were original</u> so my father <u>sat in the chair</u> while his friends, Sammy and a person whom I must now call, Mr. X, looked and touched the display.

Mr. X then took pieces of the upholstery <u>from the back outer side of the chair</u> that had Abraham Lincoln's <u>bloodstains on it </u>(not the alleged hair oil as claimed on the back inner side) and put it in his pocket after all of them looked at it.

Then according to my father there were original Abraham Lincoln's handwritten papers on a table adjacent to Abraham Lincoln's chair, which they physically picked up to read. As they went through the letters, documents and open papers they came across three to five pages as told to me by my father that they read and found shocking, so much so, that my father's friend, Mr. X, tore out these three to five pages and placed them in his pocket as he left the premise.

Fast forward now, to around 1990, when I was starting a family tree of my mother and father's family line I began asking my father questions about the Great Depression and events he witnessed during that time period.

During the many private conversations I had with my father, we would discuss events like the Hindenburg crash, which he claims he witnessed shortly after the explosion.

Furthermore, he would tell me stories about buying moonshine in Kentucky and Tennessee and fishing for sharks off the Atlantic coast.

He further told stories of gangsters, baseball players and driving Ford trucks on just buttermilk.

He told me as a furnace man he worked on Henry Ford's furnace, I believe in the Dearborn area and was fortunate enough to meet Mrs. Ford and was shown a basement room that had 70 seats for viewing movies.

The stories my father told me I found fascinating and listened to them with great interest because I knew my father, as far as I was aware of, was the last of his family line and he was my last valid source of personal information regarding the Depression era.

It was during these conversations that my father gave spontaneous utterances, without being led, of Abraham Lincoln's assassination chair and his personal papers that he read and observed his friend take.

As time passed I asked my father why didn't he ever mention these critical three to five papers to Civil War historians that he read and were taken by his friend?

The reason being, my father stated, was <u>he feared criminal reprisal</u> for his friends because they were young at the time and should not have done what they did so he remained silent throughout the years.

Though I am not an historian, yet my past and present experience has taught me that "the truth" is critical in life for survival and as stated by the greatest of all beings, "You shall know the truth and the truth shall set you free."

For in my life as a polygraph examiner I have always been in the pursuit of the truth to wherever it may lead me. Sometimes the truth was free and liberating while other times it was crushing and devastating.

So it is my desire that this book will hopefully show that I am just an investigator, whose love of my father and whose curiosity and investigative skills has forced me to delve deeper into this matter.

That said, it is also my sincere hopes and intentions by following investigative leads and collecting fragmented pieces of evidence will help to form a composite picture as if a crime scene to help me reach a correct diagnostic evaluation regarding the originality of "The Lincoln Chair" that has been at the Henry Ford Museum since 1929.

I also know that "Victory has a thousand fathers but defeat is an orphan.'

So I am prepared to be made a fool of and ostracized for it comes with the territory when seeking the truth. Yet I believe from the onset through intuition, observation, experience and common sense that <u>victory is certain</u>.

To me as a member of, "the working class" who has been controlled and forced to walk the earth beneath the scorching sun with my father, as a lowly beast of burden for "the powers" who rule here on terra firma truly believe that the only relief to those of us who can face it, <u>is the truth,</u> by whatever form or means it reveals itself to us, <u>for the truth brings change</u>.

For the truth is a weapon against "the powers", for they fear the light by cloaking themselves in darkness to conspire in secrecy.

So exposure of a perceived and possible established scam is worthy of pursuit even if it means mud will be thrown in my face.

That said, I realized certain things like this matter of the chair and the papers needed to be brought into the open from it's shrouded and dark history and reviewed with a clear mind in the public square.

To this end, I realized that my father, Edmond Ankony, now 98 years old had witnessed an event long ago that may be critical to historians or academia in general.

Still, I am uncertain if this book will be looked upon as "old news" or as being very significant with critical material.

For my father is the last of "the old ones" and his witnessing to this event that occurred at Independence Hall, Philadelphia, Pennsylvania around 1932 is relevant to knowing Abraham Lincoln's true mindset and character at the time of the Civil War.

Moreover knowing the whereabouts of this original National Treasure, "The Chair", must be made known to the public for the preservation of American history and as a rallying point for "free men" whose ancestors had shed their blood on the fields of valor for preservation of the union.

Therefore, you be my judge, but remember I am but a messenger now for two kings of which one is my father and the other is President Abraham Lincoln. Surely both of them desire that the truth be known regarding Lincoln's original written papers he wrote of which my father seen and the positive identification of the real chair of which millions of Americans want to pay respect to **be original**!

Understand please, that my investigation will be always ongoing until absolute closure is made one way or the other.

"Fiat justitia ruat caelum"

Chapter One - the Henry Ford Museum

On April 15, 2015, my wife, Denise, and I were babysitting our grandson, Anthony when our daughter, the child's mother, Tracy, stated that Henry Ford's Greenfield Village Museum, Dearborn, Michigan was having a free entrance day for family and school children.

My wife and I decided to take our grandson there to look at the vintage cars and old machines from yesteryear and to further entertain the baby's insatiable curiosity for new things.

The day was beautiful, ceiling and visibility unlimited with plenty of sunshine as we drove into the Greenfield Village (a.k.a, the Henry Ford Museum) complex.

As we placed our 1 1/2 year old grandson in his stroller we observed numerous school buses of young children heading into the museum.

Everyone was laughing and it looked like a beautiful carefree day was in front of us. We figured we would push the child around in the stroller, then eat a couple of hotdogs and fries and hoped all the activity and action would put the baby boy to sleep for a few hours.

As we walked into the main entrance building and meandered our way through the crowd of laughing children, I could hear in the distance narrators discussing certain facts about an important apparent antique or historical display that everyone was observing.

As we made our way out of the corridor entrance to the main floor of displays we walked right smack into a display of a chair that was being given great fanfare and respect.

The place was surrounded by hundreds of people and a narrator was discussing the significance of the chair in question on display. As I approached the display I quickly realized as a retired Dearborn Police sergeant that the Dearborn Police and security officials were protecting the chair.

I further realized that my wife and I had walked into something inadvertently that was of great importance to everyone who gazed upon it as we listened to the narrator discuss its chronological history and important place in American history.

When I immediately gazed upon it, I thought I knew exactly what it was due to stories that I had heard in the past, yet I had to be certain.

Upon finding out that it was Abraham Lincoln's chair in which he was assassinated in it then became apparent why there was such a commotion being drawn to this artifact.

Moreover, I found out this was the 150 year anniversary of Lincoln's assassination and people have always held Abraham Lincoln on a pedestal as almost Godlike.

I, like so many Americans loved Lincoln and looked upon him as an honest and good man who did the right thing to the best of his ability and belief for his country and people.

At this time I went up as close as I could to the chair to take pictures with a low resolution phone camera but was quickly intercepted by security and told that I was too close and had to step back. So I stepped back and shot a few low quality pictures from afar and was mad at myself that I did not have my high resolution cameras from my polygraph and private eye businesses with me.

But how was I to know?

For it was just one of those things, you make due and like my excellent Marine Corps training in my past taught me, to improvise to your situation and make a decision, so I did, by gathering as much information as I could in light of my circumstances.

As I walked back to my original location I met a Dearborn Police officer and told him the story about the chair and how it has a different meaning to me as compared to other people.

After hearing the story, he laughed then we shook hands as I departed from him.

But as my wife and I walked away, suddenly something happened to me as if out of the blue. I turned around and looked back at the large crowd of people that were mesmerized by what they were being told and I felt good and proud as always to be an American.

As I continued to look back at the chair, I realized that upon that chair sat one of the greatest presidents this country, the United States of America, has ever known.

So in all humility and as a former Marine Corps Captain, I saluted my Commander in Chief out of respect.

But Abraham Lincoln was not the only man I saluted. For I saluted another great man, my father, who is a kind and meek man that I deeply love who is still and always will be close to my heart who in the past sat in the original Abraham Lincoln chair.

As I continued looking back upon this chair from a distance I remembered the numerous stories my father had told me throughout his life of which I deeply cherished and kept them in a certain part of my heart for him and my mother only.

For they were special people, the salt of the earth kind, and God of the infinite universe in his mercy had taken my lonely and eternal drifting soul out of the infinite cosmos of time and space and placed it to be to raised, nurtured and taught by my father and mother.

During the quality time my father and I spent together I especially remembered what my dad witnessed and what he told me numerous times since about 1990 regarding his visitation to Independence Hall, Philadelphia, Pennsylvania around 1932.

My father told me that his two friends, Sammy and the other of whom I must call at this time, Mr. X had seen and made contact with the original chair that Abraham Lincoln's was assassinated in.

Moreover, at this time my father further stated that he and his friends also made physical contact with original Abraham Lincoln papers that was on display that contained Lincoln's intentions of solving and dealing with "the black problem."

After all three read these controversial Lincoln documents and realizing their historical value, Mr. X tore out three to five pages of the original Abraham Lincoln papers and kept them to himself.

As I refocused my thoughts and returned back to look at the display and brochures of the chair with all the facts and particulars about the chair, it stated that in 1929, Henry Ford, the auto magnate of Ford Motor Company acquired that chair at an auction for

$2,400 and it stayed at the Henry Ford Museum since then, except for an exhibit at Grand Rapids, Michigan and minor restoration attempts.

"That can't be?" I said to myself.

"There must be a reasonable explanation?" I said, "There must be? My father must be wrong?"

"But my father has always been an honest man?" I said to myself.

My father had nothing to gain by saying what he said and he never lied to me throughout my life, so there has to be some mix-up somewhere?

But where could the mix-up be, I wondered?

If I may digress for a moment to say my lifelong profession as with all police officers, polygraph examiners and private eyes has put us nose to nose with the criminal element and the web of deceit selfish men in high places weave to further their self-serving agenda at any cost has forced me to ask questions regarding the chair and the papers.

For my "crucible of affliction" came early in life by living on the streets of Detroit which made me no virgin to the schemes, cons, and wickedness of thieves and scoundrels, in their three piece suits with their smiling faces and deceiving handshakes, who steal from the old, the young, their family and the innocent without conscience or hesitation.

That said, as I looked back at the crowd that was mesmerized by the narrator, I couldn't help but think, "What if?" as I thought about the chair and the papers, suddenly and unexpectedly my 35 years as a state licensed polygraph interrogator in pursuit of the truth just kicked in.

Suddenly, and unexpectedly my 18 years as a state licensed private investigator/ private eye who investigates cases as an investigator kicked in.

Suddenly, and unexpectedly my 25 years as a lawman beneath the Ford Motor Company smokestacks and deployed to the "Arab Corridor" of the Dearborn Southend to study suspicious circumstances as a Dearborn Police officer kicked in.

My instincts could sense it and like a great white shark smelling blood, something didn't add up which became the demarcation point for my investigation.

For I make no claim to being a historian at all of the Civil War, Abraham Lincoln, his chair, his papers or Henry Ford, for I am an investigator and something felt wrong about the possible sanitized story being told that was worthy of pursuit and clarification.

As I stood there, my instincts and police officer's six sense could suddenly smell the possibility of "the play", and, "the big con" which I felt was in the air.

As I looked over at the innocent mothers who were trying to teach their children established and perceived truths about history yet I wondered if they themselves were unaware that they may be getting in fact duped and hoodwinked by looking at a replica instead of the original.

The fix could be in I wondered, whether done deliberately or inadvertently I thought, but how could I unravel such a mystery with no resources at my disposal to fight against this giant magnate's establishment with it's all their resources, wealth, and power.

Yet as I stood there I remembered when my father told me how he witnessed on May 26, 1937 "The Battle of the Overpass" at Ford Motor Company, gate 4, when "free men" fought against Henry Ford's goons who tried to prevent unionizing and better working conditions.

Money drove these rich magnates then and not fair play!

That said is it money that drives this institution here today and perhaps not the truth?

That thought fired me up.

For my father is the last of his kin and none now live of his birth family that remember it. For the world has changed since their passing and the truth that once was known is gone, for the truth has become myth and myth has become mired in legend.

My father, is in a sense the last of the Mohicians, the last witness to what he seen and read and what was taken on that fateful day in Independence Hall, Philadelphia Pennsylvania around 1932.

Yet, Henry Ford claimed he had the Assassination Chair of Abraham Lincoln since 1929 and it never left for Independence Hall, Philadelphia, Pennsylvania from the Henry Ford Museum as far as what is known.

As I stood there and looked at my beautiful wife, Denise, of 38 years of marriage, watching her feed our grandson, I told her the story of what I knew.

Being a practical and a very honest woman, she stated, "Abraham Lincoln's dead, there's his chair, the Civil War is over, what is there to prove? Who cares? You're wasting your time!"

I then said, "<u>The original chair of Abraham Lincoln being assassinated in cannot be in two places at the same time!</u>"

Denise looked at me inquisitively, "Are you saying to me what we are looking at here is not the original chair Abraham Lincoln was assassinated in?"

I said nothing.

Denise then stated, "Well that's a shame if people come here under a false pretense that this chair is the real deal. That's a shame if it is a replica and not the original. Your father must be wrong and got his dates mixed up?"

"Imagine", I said, "Since 1929 how many people have seen this chair?"

"That's a shame", Denise said, "A real shame. Can you prove it?"

I looked at baby Anthony eating a cookie and stated, "I don't know and I don't know if I want too?

All I know is, my father has nothing to gain by telling me what he did and seen. Yet this institution on the 150 year anniversary of the assassination of Abraham Lincoln has millions to gain."

As Denise looked at me, she stated, "Richard, who cares? Who cares about this chair or that chair, the Civil War is over, it's the way it is. Nothing can change now."

I said nothing, but the words of Pontius Pilot came to my mind, "The truth. What is the truth?"

The matter was then dropped and I decided right then and there to gather information of the particulars of this matter from my father again and hopefully his story would be flawed, end of story.

But it didn't end.

It began.

<u>I now state in advance, I am not fingering or bad mouthing anyone throughout this book specifically but the sequence of events, chain of custody/chain of evidence regarding the chair are questionable at best and I needed to bring closure on this matter, one way or another, for my father's honor and word is at stake</u>.

Chapter Two - My Father's Story

"Behold, a messenger I send before you to discuss matters of state, strike him not, least I destroy your kingdom in a fortnight."

The Warning - author unknown

In the following days I thought about Abraham Lincoln's chair and during my walks I questioned myself about getting involved in this matter for the words of my wife kept coming back to me, "Who cares?"

But after talking with my father numerous times in the old age home, I was troubled and saddened by the conditions good men and women are compelled to live in.

Finally, I thought I should at least tell my father's side of the story regarding the original Abraham Lincoln's chair and his original personal papers.

My father consistently maintained his story and was insistent about what he observed around 1932 at Independence Hall, Philadelphia, Pennsylvania.

As I thought about my father in his health care center and this imprisonment of him, against his wishes and mine, I felt terrible of his helpless state, which is an unfitting place for my dad of sane mind.

I was deeply troubled by observing the collection of broken worn-out bodies that were like prisoners on death row awaiting their final sentence from "The Reaper", at the end of their road.

As I looked upon these elderly people, once of distinguished statue, as they sat there in diapers with minds like little children holding baby dolls, I remembered the words of my beloved mother, "You come into this world with nothing Richard and you leave with nothing."

How true it is I thought.

The smell of feces, urine and vomit overwhelmed me at times and the helplessness of broken bodies starring out into deep space often left me feeling depressed when I left the health care center.

However to my surprise, which made me feel good, I notice when I talked with my father about the Abraham Lincoln assassination chair he became alive again as if he was Lazarus rising from the dead. When my father and I discussed the chair and the papers I was left with the impression that my father left the ether world he was dumped in and returned back to me into the world of the living by contributing something again to society as a whole.

My father told me numerous times he thought this was a worthwhile endeavor by bringing the truth into the limelight which made me feel good to see him happy and vibrant again.

Still at times it was hard for me to face the hard, cold truth and the dirty low-down of what circumstances put my father in this dungeon.

Yet, I knew firsthand from years of experience in the field of criminology that the criminal mind of some "regressive and unevolved" people bordered on complete demonic possession who purposely and without conscience hurt and deliberately destroy other peoples lives just to further their greedy and diabolical existence. How deep must hell be to hide their shame?

Yet I was forced to keep an open mind and accept, at least for now, that my father will not roam the earth as a free man anymore.

Realizing this, I thought to myself, should I not stand with my father, right or wrong, and try to prove his story, as he wanted me to do?

For he isn't heavy Father, he is my father.

For this story is not just about a chair or papers of worth.

No, it is about the possibility of distorting the truth with guilty knowledge and then deliberately misleading the innocent masses out of millions of dollars.

If this is true, it is criminal in nature.

If it is not true, then I will and must play the fool by taking my fathers and my lashings at the post in the public square before the duped minions and paid lackeys as the "Hunchback of Notre Dame."

Power brokers who will <u>knowingly</u> and gladly feed the unsuspecting innocent, replicas, and disguise it as originals, for profit look at us as a senseless mob of dumb down cannon fodder to be swindled and expended, until you catch them!

Yes, I answered, I will fight my father's battle come hell or high water!

My father's story started about 25 years ago around 1990 when my dad and I would discuss old times during the depression.

My father told me stories of the Great Depression when he would drive old Ford Model-T trucks to sell watermelons with his father. When they would run out of gas they would run the truck on buttermilk where apparently the fat of the milk would burn so good it acted like nitro.

He also told me how he would buy moonshine on the back roads of Kentucky where he would place a quarter on a log and within a half hour a jug of moonshine would suddenly appear.

He further told me how he had seen the Hindenburg explosion about a half hour after it occurred at Naval Air Station, Lakehurst, New Jersey. Also, how he watched bi-planes drop Baby Ruth's candy bars on the kids playing in the park in Michigan City, Indiana as they ran helter skelter in the streets and on rooftops to get the candy while their mothers yelled at them.

As I listened intently like a young schoolboy to my father's stories, one story kept coming to the forefront as my father described intricate details about a witnessed event that occurred around 1932 in Independence Hall, Philadelphia, Pennsylvania.

My father told me at least ten times as I recall since about 1990 a story that really stuck with me about his friend Sammy, Mr. X and himself who were visiting family in Philadelphia, Pennsylvania around 1932.

(Please Note: Due to possible legal and criminal complications in the making of this book, I had to change the original name to Mr. X because the word "taken" was referred to as "steal."

That said, for fear of criminal prosecution and knowing the law from both sides, I had to retract the real name at this time.

Yet the true purpose of this book is about revealing the truth to the best of my ability about the original Lincoln chair and the original Lincoln papers and not about intimidating a 98 year old man with a jail sentence.)

At that time, my father and his friends decided to go to Independence Hall, Philadelphia, Pennsylvania to look at the Liberty Bell and other historical documents of the United States and relics from our founding fathers.

As they entered into the complex near the Liberty Bell, there was Abraham Lincoln's original "Assassination Chair" next to a table containing original Abraham Lincoln's papers.

As they approached the chair and papers, my father stated in those days things were not protected and people could and did handle these important historical documents and antiques. on a regular basis.

It was no big deal back then and from time to time people would mischievously, without criminal intent, "take" but not "steal" antiques as souvenirs.

My father stated the guardians of these critical historical artifacts were asleep at the wheel and neglectful of their duties by not protecting the artifacts better.

Basically my father stated they, the security, were not around for the most part and visiting guests were left to their own discretions on how to handle the sacred archives.

Immediately, my father <u>sat</u> in the original Abraham Lincoln's assassination chair for a brief period of time.

During this particular occasion, Mr. X took <u>pieces</u> from the <u>back outer side</u> of Abraham's Lincolns chair of which, as my father described, contained blood and not hair oil as alleged on the back inner side.

Furthermore, the three young men <u>read</u> the original Abraham Lincoln documents that were placed next to the chair on a table and found three to five pages, according to my father, to be alarming and contrary to their understanding of freedom for the black race.

They were so alarmed that, Mr. X, decided to take these three to five original Abraham Lincoln documents from a pile of open papers that had been placed on an adjacent desk and put them in his pocket.

My father then said, that one of the papers, at a later time, was sold for five dollars by Mr. X, which was a lot of money during the depression. But Mr. X kept the other two to four pages for himself.

After I heard the story from my father, a while later in the Detroit Free Press around 1990-1995 on page "One A" or page "One B", an article appeared about two inches by two inches in the lower right-hand corner of the page, which read to the effects, that a professional historian or historians were asking the public for help and if anyone was aware of certain critical papers from Lincoln's notes or diary that were missing.

The way it was worded, as I recall at the time, left me with the impression that these papers taken by Mr. X were the papers in question being looked for by the historians.

Though I could be mistaken that the historians were looking instead for other missing Lincoln papers, I felt intuitively that the papers Mr. X took were the papers in question that the historians were desperately searching for.

Regrettably, I did not keep the article because it wasn't important to me at the time, yet I remembered the article distinctly.

Furthermore, I did not respond to the historians in question who were urgently looking for the missing Lincoln papers due to the fact that my elderly father did not want trouble to be brought to his doorstep. So I kept quiet about the matter until now.

So this is where I stand today.

What I am being told is a witnessed event that occurred around 1932 in Independence Hall, Philadelphia, Pennsylvania where my father has stated to me consistently that he witnessed pieces of the original Abraham Lincoln assassination chair being taken and that he witnessed and read certain original Abraham Lincoln papers taken which contained matters involving the black race which was to occur at the end of the Civil War of which they found alarming at that time and so did I presently.

Despite that witnessed event in 1932 by my father and his friends, Henry Ford, the auto magnate, claimed he had the original Abraham Lincoln chair since 1929 in Henry Ford Greenfield Village behind a glass cage.

Now according to an article from the Detroit News, Lincoln's final chair comes out from behind glass, by Greg Tasker, April 8, 2015, it states that "Except for

21

conservation efforts and transport to an exhibit in Grand Rapids, Michigan, a few years back, Lincoln's chair has rarely been out of it's glass enclosure since it arrived at Greenfield Village in 1930."

Knowing that the original chair could not be at two places at once, I had to investigate further.

So I decided first to investigate my father's claim by interrogating him in depth to gather more details on this matter.

Though I am certain as a polygraph examiner of 35 years my father would have passed a polygraph examination regarding this matter, I felt the rigors of such an exam with his health as such was unfeasible at this time.

So I decided that despite my father's bad hearing and poor eyesight I would interview him among the noise and chaos of an old age home. And chaotic it was with the peering eyes of snoops and unwanted intrusions by staff and nomadic drifters.

Nevertheless, I pushed forward and hoped my father would break and give me an inconsistent story and this matter before me would end without incident.

Against this backdrop, I decided to ask repeatedly *certain relevant core questions over and over again* so as to reach a high level of consistency where I knew beyond a reasonable doubt, that my father's story was true.

Remember consistency is conducive and indicative of truthfulness.

For I didn't want critics, if they were to comment, to say that my father misunderstood the questions I was asking him due to his partial deafness or I was leading him to a favorable response.

Seeing that a polygraph examination I could not administer to my 98 year old father for health reasons and most probably against medical protocol, I had to reach a diagnostic opinion that I was comfortable with which would withstand the rigors of mainstream media if this book by chance should go viral.

Though in truth, I felt this booklet would probably just die on the vine and perhaps just twenty or so books would be sold because who reads nowadays or gives a damn about a chair, even if it is Abraham Lincoln's.

I didn't mind that because I felt only the professional historian or curators would be interested in this book, if at all.

So PLEASE understand that repeated critical questions were asked over and over to help increase the probability that my father's story was consistent and he was telling the truth.

When I looked at this case as a polygraph examiner it had all the makings of a domestic violence/marriage infidelity type examination of which I was very experienced in and familiar with, that is, "He said. She said" which was without any additional witnesses or evidence.

So in essence then, this case figuratively speaking got down to a heavyweight fight, that is, Henry Ford vs. Edmond Ankony and my money was on my father.

So it was important then that I try everything to break the impasse between them.

I realized the tiebreaker could happen if I sent a letter to Independence Hall in the blind regarding if the original Abraham Lincoln's Chair or his original papers were ever there?

I felt, or shall I say believed, that the Independence Hall Museum, staff members, must have <u>excellent records on a daily basis of what entered and left their national museum at any given time.</u>

I further felt that Independence Hall could tell me with <u>absolute certainty the exact time and date that this chair or **National Treasure** was present at their location or tell me otherwise.</u>

However when I received a professional response from the head national curator (God bless her) at Independence Hall, Philadelphia, Pennsylvania, her answer was very surprising which thickened the plot.

I then realized that I had to keep going because things were just not adding up and as Judge Judy would say, "If it don't make sense, it didn't happen!"

And the Henry Ford Museum, Abraham Lincoln assassination chair's story just didn't make sense, which led me to believe that there was more to this story.

Chapter 3 - The Chair's Story

In the following days I gathered more and more information regarding "The Chair" and as best as I could determine, the story of Abraham Lincoln's assassination chair is filled with intrigue and mystery.

The paper trail and chain of evidence of this **National Treasure** almost from the very beginning is in question.

Speaking collectively as a lawman, polygraph examiner and private eye and in my sincere opinion how could we have allowed ourselves to be perhaps duped liked this?

What is being peddled to us, "the masses" regarding the originality of this chair since the day Abraham Lincoln was murdered in it, I believe is pure nonsense.

I cannot believe the guardians of this **National Treasure,** who are professionals, do not feel the way I do, for one does not have to be an attorney, a judge or jury to see this for what it is.

I believe and will state right now in the open that there is a high probability around 75% or more that a "replica" or "relic" is being sold to the public as an "original" at the Henry Ford Museum based on the case facts available.

Remember, that chair at the Henry Ford Museum is being advertised as "100% original" while I find it to be 75% or higher "a replica" or a "relic."

After looking at "The Chair's" history I cannot and will not change my beliefs or findings even if the Henry Ford Museum comes up with some hidden knowledge known only to them about the chair.

To me, any hidden knowledge now revealed about the chair I will find suspicious and questionable at this time, which is why my father and I decided to publish this book on the run.

For my position right now is, that the Henry Ford Museum will have to admit after 85 years of displaying their Abraham Lincoln's chair that they are selling to the public as original may not be so.

Just like the original chair cannot be at two places at the same time, the Henry Ford Museum and I cannot both be right.

Therefore I present my case to the public at large and let them be the judge.

Moreover, and in my further opinion "the best of the best curators" in this country must wonder among themselves, if not within their private circles, that the authenticity of the chair at Greenfield Village is questionable at best and doubtful at worst.

In my opinion the chair is used as a circus staple to draw uninformed masses as a tourist attraction for purely monetary reasons by proclaiming that the Lincoln assassination chair at Henry Ford Museum-Greenfield Village is "original."

So let me give you the story, in the following pages, as best as I can gather from word of mouth, valid articles, the internet, my father, comments from a professional curator and all my years in the investigative field.

Abraham Lincoln as we all know was assassinated on Good Friday, April 14, 1865 where Harry Clay Ford, the theater manager of the Ford Theater, owned the chair that Lincoln was assassinated in. The chair was taken from Harry Ford's residence from a suite or set.

It appears that the chair was taken from Harry Ford's suite that was part of a set. Seeing that Harry Ford was a theater manager of the Ford Theater, the word "set" may well imply "theatrical scenery" which means the chair may well have been part of a theatrical scenery set. Which would then imply there may have been more then one chair of this type in the theater as later confirmed in this book by a highly regarded expert furniture maker hired by the United States Government.

Though I have little understanding on how furniture is made I am unaware of ever hearing or seeing, as far as I know, a chair that is "The one and only type chair of it's kind." For my experience has shown me that when a chair is made perhaps hundreds if not thousands of the same type of chair is also made.

I find it strange that expert historians, as far as I know, never asked the question, "Is this Lincoln assassination chair the one and only type of this kind made?"

If the answer came back yes, then why wasn't this critical fact of information known prior?

If the answer came back no, that is, many chairs were made, then to me any reasonable and prudent person can see that the Henry Ford Museum needs to do some explaining in the public square.

Now Harry Clay Ford is not related to the auto magnate, Henry Ford, though their last names are the same.

When Abraham Lincoln was assassinated the War Department, on April 22, 1865, seven days after Lincoln died seized "the chair" for evidence and to further <u>prevent souvenir hunters from taking pieces of the chair.</u>

As I understand, at this time the Federal government purchased the now closed Ford Theater for $100,00, which included all the contents within the theater including "The Chair."

Guards had to be posted 24/7 to protect and preserve the Ford Theater and "The Chair" in the presidential box due to it being a crime scene.

Yet despite the total guarded protection of this crime scene, pieces of the chair had been torn, ripped and the chair was "mutilated" by souvenir takers.

After hearing of such reckless abandonment of protecting the crime scene and the damage that was incurred by "The Chair", Assistant Secretary of War Charles Dana ordered "The Chair" removed to better protective custody.

Moreover, Assistant Secretary of War Charles Dana was allegedly so enraged at what he had heard of "The Chair" being "mutilated" at this national crime scene in full view of the protective guards, he ordered the imprisonment of anyone who was in charge of protecting the presidential box!

This directive by the Assistant Secretary of War to "imprison personnel" assigned to protect this critical evidence for trial due to the severe damage or stated "mutilation" already incurred by "The Chair" is serious business and further reveals the secretary's rage.

This order by the Assistant Secretary of War "to imprison" is also a very strong indicator right from the onset of Lincoln's assassination of the severe damage already incurred by "The Chair", while guarded under orders.

It had to be a known national disgrace and when the Assistant Secretary of War <u>wants imprisonment</u> for those who were entrusted to protect this **National Treasure** from the public for evidence of a crime scene, the damage of the chair had to be severe.

Speaking as a former Marine Corps Captain with a platoon of Marines under my authority and as a former police patrol sergeant with a platoon of police officers under my command, I know that my "ass is done like dinner" if I was in charge of that detail when "The Chair" was damaged and the Assistant Secretary of War is calling for imprisonment.

Buffalo chips flow down hill and I am certain I would have lost my military commission, been terminated, publicly disgraced and given a dishonorable discharge.

<u>So therefore this "order" is very important for many reasons, one of which is that right from the beginning within seven days after Abraham Lincoln dies, "The Chair" is already torn and "mutilated" even while fully protected.</u>

Now what this states is that if "The Chair" right from the beginning is assaulted with pieces stripped from it for souvenirs while under guarded protection and within seven days of Abraham Lincoln being shot <u>then what in God's name would happen to this chair if it was unguarded and unprotected for 64 years so much so, that even the rightful owner in 1928 did not know where the chair was?</u>

Moreover, people of the day were aware of the importance of "The Chair" and if they did strip pieces of it while guarded would they not steal or switch the chair for another similar chair while it is unguarded?

I don't think this is a far fetched theory for the world I work in is an infestation of low life's, scoundrels, thieves and the dregs of society, <u>this is a no brainer</u>, consider it gone!

So nearly right from the very beginning of the chairs journey "The Chair's" originality must be scrutinized and held in question.

After the trial of the trial conspirators, "The Chair" held by the War Department, is sent over to the Department of the Interior in 1867 for safekeeping. The chair is received by Interior Secretary O.H. Browning who <u>acknowledges receipt of the chair</u> by stating, "It will afford me satisfaction to have the Chair deposited in the proper place, among other <u>relics,</u> in this Department for safekeeping."

During my investigation and henceforth I did not find anyone stating on the record any official acknowledgement for <u>receipt of the chair</u>. This would explain to me why as will be read later in this book why the owner of the chair in 1928 did not know where the chair was.

Another interesting point is Interior Secretary O.H. Browning referring to the chair as a relic? Perhaps it's just a misspoken word or perhaps it is implying only part of the chair is still intact.

Shortly thereafter "The Chair" shows up at the Patent Office building for about two years from around 1867-1869 where it is first put on <u>public display</u> as an exhibit.

So it is exposed to the public again and it stands to reason if "The Chair" was "mutilated" even after being guarded as evidence then whether guarded or unguarded pieces of upholstery were being taken.

Now in 1869, "The Chair" gets sent over to the Smithsonian Institute and is put in storage, "<u>the exact whereabouts is held a closely guarded secret</u>."

What does "a closely guarded secret" mean?

This means that "The Chair" is now protected from people, the elements, and within a secure premise "for your eyes only."

While at the Smithsonian Institute "The Chair" is placed in a warehouse for 24 years, until 1893, where it is neglected and used as some kind of door stop or lunch chair and receives water damage and alleged hair grease on the back upper portion of the inner chair by people sitting on it.

This begs the question again, if "The Chair" when guarded had pieces taken from it by souvenir hunters in April 1865, now four years later, is it safe to assume that when "The Chair" is unguarded for the next 24 years that pieces of the chair were also taken or perhaps "The Chair" itself was taken?

I believe that it is again reasonable to conclude that numerous pieces of the chair were taken from this unguarded and unprotected chair and that the chair at this time was stolen, damaged, destroyed, lost or switched.

I further remind you that "The Chair" was suppose to be protected from the public's eye and physical contact at the Smithsonian Institute, instead it was abandoned in their warehouse, sustained further damage by being left unguarded and unprotected and ravaged by the Smithsonian employees and their associates.

Now this alleged guarded **National Treasure,** in 1893, some 24 years later in a unprotected warehouse is then taken from it's alleged protected habitat and safe sanctuary of a soiled unguarded warehouse operated by a national museum, The Smithsonian Institute and sent on loan to a Lincoln museum collector, Osborn Oldroyd, in Washington D.C.

Now remember at the Smithsonian Institute the alleged "The Chair" whereabouts was supposedly a closely guarded secret and deliberately kept from the prying eyes and hands of the public yet despite that the chair was neglected and unprotected from the elements and Smithsonian employees for 24 years.

Now the chair is sent to a museum to be put on display before the public again for the next four years 1893-1897 where obviously it becomes exposed and unprotected from the public where the elements and perhaps vandalism damage the chair even further.

Which begs the question, "Why would an alleged protected chair kept in secret for 24 years at the Smithsonian Institute and be left unprotected only to be sent to a place to be exposed and unprotected again before the public for four more years?

It doesn't make sense."

Then, the alleged "The Chair" is then taken from the exposed elements and is then returned back to the National Smithsonian Museum around 1897 where it is put in unprotected storage again.

Now, five years later in 1902, the alleged "The Chair" is finally given after 37 years, a unique "Accession number-38912 and was catalogued in the Department of Anthropology.

This number is a unique number given to each new acquisition as it is entered in the catalog of a library or museum.

Which further begs the question, "Why in God's name did this alleged "The Chair" take 37 years to receive a unique identifier number, so it could be identified?"

Is the Smithsonian Institute now stating that the Abraham Lincoln assassination chair after 37 years is not unique in itself by visual observation?

I mean "The Chair" went without identification for 37 years, so why now?

Perhaps the concern was that officials were aware that there were other chairs of this nature floating around for it did come from a set and a suite?

Again, people knew from the very beginning that Abraham Lincoln's chair was important and if they knew it was important they also knew it was worth money and if it was worth money and is unprotected then someone most probably already stole it by now.

If that isn't gross mismanagement or asleep at the wheel then what is?

So what I believe was identified at this time was "A Chair" and not "The Chair."

So what we have here is "A Chair" that has been identified with a unique identifier-38912 that is now purported to be "The Chair" after 37 years of total neglect.

If pieces of "The Chair" were taken within seven days of the assassination when it was heavily guarded most probably by Union troops, it becomes self-evident then that the value of "The Chair" was known immediately from the beginning.

If this is so, then greedy money hungry "money changers" of the day could have easily made a switch for sure for it was not outside their capacity or capabilities to fabricate another chair.

I am certain that I am not the only one who thinks this way especially prior to the identifier being put in place and perhaps even afterwards.

So now, this alleged, "A Chair" has a unique identifier and whether it is "The Chair" or not at this time is still in question.

Though I am fairly certain at this point if this were a criminal trial and the chair was brought in as evidence based on it's ambiguous prior paper trail and questionable chain of evidence/chain of custody it would have been severely criticized by the standing judge and most probably thrown out at the door.

The "A Chair" is now back in storage at the Smithsonian Museum for another 31 more years where it is left in a warehouse supposedly in secret where it was again abused even with it's unique identifier by the elements and people at the Smithsonian Institute until 1928.

Now in 1928, Blanche Chapman Ford, the widow of Harry Ford, who was the original owner of "The Chair" from the Ford Theater where Lincoln was murdered at writes a letter to the Smithsonian Institute curator, Theodore Belote, regarding the chair.

Mrs. Blanche Chapman Ford asks in her letter these incredible questions to Theodore Belote.

"Is it true that you have the chair?" and, **"If so, will you kindly tell me why it is not on display?"**

Now mind you, Blanche Chapman Ford, Harry Ford's widowed wife, has now inherited and become the rightful owner of the original "The Chair."

So the question is, "Why doesn't Blanche Chapman Ford know where her chair is at?"

What happened to the chain of evidence/chain of custody of keeping the owner of this **National Treasure** informed of the chair's whereabouts?

If the owner doesn't know where her valued property is at, nor is aware of its whereabouts, then who would know?

If no one knows then this is one more added proof that "The Chair" has already been misappropriated.

Urban legend has it that the curator Theodore Belote was an ardent supporter of the Confederacy and former son of a slave owner who did not want to have Abraham Lincoln's chair displayed for it would portray Abraham Lincoln as a martyr.

Forgive me, now that theory is pure "Buffalo Chips."

Why?

First, Lincoln was already a martyr.

Second, the historians are trying to say, this one man, a curator with ruffled feathers did not want to show "The Chair" for personal reasons.

However, the Smithsonian Institute is a national museum and the Civil War was over for 63 years. This curator had to have more sense then this for if one is in charge of a national museum then one must think on a national level.

The curator has first an obligation to the American People and not to his own subjected personal vendetta or agenda.

Moreover, if this were so, Belote would not have been placed as curator in that distinguished institution and fired forthwith upon this revelation.

As a lawman for twenty-five years, when evidence or property of another is seized, a numbered receipt or a report number is given with details of the property being taken and where it is to be placed with all the specific details as to why that particular object in question is seized and by whom taken.

But here in 1928 a **National Treasure** of significant importance since 1865, that is 63 years later, it's positive whereabouts is unknown to the owner!

And if she doesn't know in 1928 where this **National Treasure** is or has been when the Smithsonian received it back in 1869, then surely no curator or historian would know either with certainty!

Now the Bill of Rights states in Amendment five that no person shall be deprived of life liberty or property without due process of law, nor shall private property be taken for public use without just compensation.

Well the chair was private and taken due to a capital crime in 1865 and up until 1928 there was no compensation given. So it appears the government lost track of the chair and could not give money for something they knew not where it was just like the owner.

But the kicker comes from the second question, which is as blinding as the first, when Mrs. Blanche Chapman Ford then asks, **"Will you kindly tell me why it is not on display?"**

Imagine that?

Well, lets go back.

The Patent Office building already had it on display / exhibit for only a year or two, and in 1869 the item is delivered to the Smithsonian Institute to be put in storage, the exact whereabouts a closely held secret.

The Smithsonian Institute takes it out of secrecy and sends it to be on display in 1893 to the Lincoln museum collector, *Osborn Oldroyd*, where it stayed for the next four years and obviously was exposed to the public, the elements and perhaps vandalism.

It, the alleged "The Chair" is then taken from the elements and is then returned back to the National Smithsonian Institute around 1897 where it was most probably held again in a secret location for "your eyes only."

So prior to Mrs. Blanche Chapman Ford asking the question in 1928, **"Will you kindly tell me why it is not on display?"** it has already been on display at least twice of which the curators of the Smithsonian Institute must have been aware of.

So why not put it on display at the Smithsonian Institute for they already sent it out to other locations to be exposed to the elements and people?

So the "historical theorist" alleged answer was, that the curator at the time who was in charge of the Smithsonian Institute, was the son of a former slave owner and Abraham Lincoln was not his favorite, so he didn't put it on display. Supposedly, the curator of the museum claimed because the chair was directly connected with such a horrible and deplorable event he wouldn't display it.

Hmmm, let's see here, first the Smithsonian allegedly keeps the chair in absolute secrecy since 1869 yet they are instrumental in sending it for public exposure to other museums for display where it is manhandled and further damaged.

Furthermore, they don't inform the rightful owner of this **National Treasure** where "The Chair" is, or who has it for that matter and as a matter of common courtesy they don't even give a reasonable answer as to why it is not on display.

When confronted the curator comes back with a questionable and suspicious answer which was "The Chair" was directly connected with such a horrible and deplorable event so it wouldn't be put on display.

My take at this juncture point is that the Smithsonian Institute curator got <u>"called out" and didn't know where the damn chair was, so he gave a stupid alibi!</u>

Whether "The Chair" was stolen, destroyed or misplaced on his watch, he didn't know and apparently nor did he care. So when he got "called out" by Mrs. Blanche Chapman Ford, he, the curator panicked and got another chair and put the same identifier on it and sent it to her.

Then in the winter of 1929 the alleged "A Chair" perceived by the public as "The Chair", which is a million dollar item for someone, is put on the auction block, and sold for a mere $2,400 to Israel Sack, who hands it over to Henry Ford, the automotive magnate, whose museum, "The Henry Ford Museum-Greenfield Village" just happened to be opening that year and a tourist attraction draw was needed.

So the perceived "The Chair" which could and did make millions for a museum owner such as Henry Ford gets "The Chair" for a meager $2,400 dollars over other bidders who no doubt must have also have known this chair was a "cash cow."

My take on this as to why would a highly valued item as the Lincoln chair be purchased at such a measly price that could draw millions of dollars in tourism is this.

My answer is simple, because it wasn't "The Chair", it was "A Chair" and the players or the bidders knew it!!

Remember, to Henry Ford, "The Chair" or "A Chair" is a huge money maker, for in either case, Mr. Ford knew that what was important is what the public perceives as the truth and not the truth. So since 1929 after 85 years at the Henry Ford Museum the public still perceives "A CHAIR" as "THE CHAIR"!

Then Henry Ford, further covers "the play" by throwing up a smoke screen by attempting to show a continuing chain of evidence/chain of custody and paper trail of the alleged "The Chair" arriving at Greenfield Village with some grainy movie, (You Tube "Unpacking Lincoln's Chair 1929") that looks worst then the old RKO movie, "The Thing."

Now, the alleged "The Chair" has sat at the Henry Ford-Greenfield Village except for minor touch-ups and displayed once at Grand Rapids, Michigan and has never left the museum or the State of Michigan for that matter since 1929.

Yet about three years later, around 1932, at Independence Hall, Philadelphia, Pennsylvania that housed numerous **National Treasures** and is certainly a higher and a more prestigious museum then "The Henry Ford Museum", in walks my now 98 year old father with his two friends who see and make physical contact with the original "The Chair."

Low and behold in front of their eyes sits, according to the placards, is the original "The Chair" of Abraham Lincoln that he was assassinated in.

They take a 2"x 3" piece of upholstery from the back outer side of the original Abraham Lincoln chair and take some original papers that Abraham Lincoln wrote that was on a table next to the chair.

My father and his friends sit in "The Chair."

You say, "Your kidding?"

I say, "Nope, straight scoop!"

So now, I am faced with a scenario of "Whose your Daddy?"

Though more of this matter will be discussed later in the book, what should a professional investigator do?

Well, the first order of business is to interrogate my dear Dad further, he must have it wrong....he must?

But since around 1990 when I first recalled my father telling me this story he never once changed his story line. Despite that I will interrogate him anyway to further confirm his veracity.

Then the next order of business would be to send an e-mail to Independence Hall with the hopes of getting an answer from a reputable source.

Though I didn't think I would get a reply, to my surprise I did get a response from a high ranking professional where her answer surprised me.

The head curator of Independence Hall (*Bless her heart*) sends a response that puts my head in a tailspin.

The National curator states that at that time around 1932, the City of Philadelphia managed Independence Hall and "the records that <u>survived</u> of that management were <u>spotty at best!</u>"

What the hell does that mean?

You mean there is no definitive answer?

That is, cutting to the quick, no one knows one way or the other.

Their answer at best therefore could only be speculation, that is, maybe, maybe not, possibly, possibly not, probably, probably not, likely, unlikely, certainly, certainly not.

Therefore those in the know have no way to verify with certainty that "The Chair" and "The Papers" were either there or not there?

So I stated this to my father, "Dad it has been stated by someone "in the know" that it is <u>unlikely</u> that there were original Abraham Lincoln papers there at Independence

Hall at the time you were there. Moreover, it was further stated and <u>seriously doubted</u> that the Lincoln Chair was ever there."

Upon hearing this my father got madder then hell, because he felt his honor and integrity was being questioned and he told me to this effect, "Richard, they'll (referring to authorities in general and no one specific) change the records because of their embarrassment of not telling the truth all these years to the public, so publish the book on the fly."

My Dad felt those guardians overlooking "The Chair" really didn't know where the chair was absolutely, just like the "Holy Grail" or the "Ark of the Covenant" and my father believed a possible public uproar of being taken for so many years could occur.

I then said, "I will do this for you dad if that's your wish, but I don't know if the book will even sell, for like my wife says, who cares?"

He then replied immediately, "Publish it, Richard!"

So now, suddenly everything became "urgent" and I was forced to publish on the fly without all the proper editing and extensive reviewing of this book prior to publication.

I now had to publish this book and revise it, if need be, with a second edition, etc., before as my father perceived, "<u>The powers come up with a story line to cover themselves</u>."

So my mission now was to expose this situation and as a prior "whistleblower" in my past and not virgin or fearful of the courts, I would launch this book on the run.

You see my problem now?

So as I am finishing up this book for publication I then find this article.

Taken from an article of the Observer/News: <u>Shocker: There's a Confederate Flag Sewn Into Lincoln's Chair at Ford's Theatre</u> by Joe Lapointe on 06/29/15.

The Ford Theater where Lincoln was shot in was being renovated in the mid-1960's in Washington, D.C.

At this time <u>our government</u> decided that they needed to make a replica of Lincoln's assassination chair at the theater so as to perfect the display scene of Abraham Lincoln's final moments of his life.

So while the Ford Theater, a popular and compelling tourist attraction run by the National Park Service was being renovated, our government asked to measure Abraham Lincoln's assassination chair at the Henry Ford Museum where it was held since 1929, as the alleged original, so it would allow them to build an exact replica of the scene at the Ford Theater.

The Henry Ford Museum refused!

When the rebuilt Ford Theater finally reopened in 1968, the builder of the replica chair for the theater, a now-deceased craftsman named Carlton McLendon was forced to worked off of photographs of "The Chair" taken right after the assassination of Abraham Lincoln from the Library of Congress.

This had to be done this way because of the Henry Ford Museum's refusal to let the United States Government or McLendon inspect their alleged "The Chair."

McLendon told Nancy Barnhouse of the Cleveland Plain Dealer that he also **found a chair just like Lincoln's among family furniture pieces** and that he used it as a model.

As it's been prior stated "The Chair" was taken from a suite and a set in 1865!

I am sure the Henry Ford Museum has a proper political and sanitized answer as to why they said no to the United States Government of which they made billons off of during World War II, the Korean War and the then ongoing Vietnam War.

But from my standpoint I see something totally different and what I see is this.

In my opinion, the Henry Ford Museum refused the United States Government permission because they were concerned that what Henry Ford was hiding from the public since 1929 would be revealed and that upon inspection of the chair by government experts, especially Carlton McLendon, they would find that "The Chair", Henry Ford was alluding to hold as an original was in fact, "A Chair" that was an altered version or replica of the original version and the specifications were not correct.

The only proof Henry Ford has showed so far in the chain of evidence was a grainy movie in 1929 of a box containing "A Chair" marked Henry Ford Museum that had as much clarity in resolution as an old RKO movie.

Secondly, as I stated prior Abraham Lincoln assassination chair was from a set or suite of furniture.

Now low and behold, Carlton McLendon, the expert furniture craftsmen finds a chair just like Lincoln's Chair in the Ford Theater.

So we now know for sure that there are at least four Abraham Lincoln assassination type chairs floating around!

Chapter 4- Correspondence with the Curator of Independence Hall

To: Independence Hall   June 3, 2015

From: Richard Ankony

My 98-year-old father was witness to certain original Abraham Lincoln papers being taken and also parts of the Assassination Chair of Abraham Lincoln being taken. He states that this event occurred between 1932 and 1939 in Independence Hall. Could you please tell me if Independence Hall has ever had the Lincoln Assassination chair on display between these years? I am attempting to shed light on what I perceive to be a critical historical event on the content of the papers and your assistance in this matter would be greatly appreciated.

Thank you in advance.

Richard Ankony

****

From NPS.gov: Abraham Lincoln missing papers and Assassination Chair

From :Diethorn, Karie

To: Richard Ankony

CC

Renee Albertoli

Jun 5 at 12:03 PM

9.D (INDE)

Mr. Ankony--

I'm happy to look into your questions. To assist me, would you clarify a few things:

When you say that your father saw "certain original Abraham Lincoln papers taken", do you mean that he saw someone steal them and "parts of the Assassination Chair?"

By "Assassination Chair", do you mean the chair that Lincoln sat in at Ford's Theater on the night that he was shot?

What do you mean by "a critical historical event on the content of the papers?" What "event" and what "content?"

Thanks for this additional information.

Karie Diethorn

Chief Curator

Independence National Historical Park

National Park Service

US Department of the Interior

143 S. 3rd Street

Philadelphia PA 19106

phone 215-XXX-XXXX

fax 215-XXX-XXXX

cell 610-XXX-XXXX

****

TO: Mrs. Karie Diethorn

From: Richard Ankony June 5, 2015

I sincerely want to thank you for your timely response for in fact I thought I was not going to get any.

That said, I don't know how to go forward with this matter though I want too but based on the word you use "steal" has thrown up flags.

If I may digress for a moment, I am a retired 25-year lawman, a police sergeant out of Dearborn, Michigan. I have about six books out on the Internet and my credentials are stated if you type my name, Richard Ankony, under Google or Yahoo.

However this matter is not about selling my books that are already out there but may well involve a book I am in the works of publishing.

Moreover, this matter is not about notoriety, I don't need it and don't want it.

First and foremost I am not a historian by the farthest stretch of the imagination for I am a state licensed investigator and state licensed polygraph interrogator besides being a retired lawman.

What this matter is about in brief, and forgive me for talking encrypted, I realized after hearing a certain story numerous times that someone was the last survivor to a witnessed event and that the contents of what was witnessed, though hearsay now, I felt and I repeat, I felt was alarming to say the least.

I am uncertain if it is all garbage and wish it was, though I believe it is not.

The choice I had to make as a pursuer of the truth was to let it die on the vine or shed light on it. That is, it is not my problem! But my conscience got the better of me and this great country of ours was worthy of the truth despite how good or ugly this information may or may not be.

Proceeding with caution now and to answer your first question, material was observed taken regarding Abraham Lincoln's papers and Assassination Chair.

The papers were read and the contents based on my opinion was disturbing.

Regarding, your second question, the chair I am discussing was the original Abraham Lincoln's chair that he was assassinated on.

To answer the third question, "critical event" it appears, though again I am not a historian of Abraham Lincoln, his intentions of what to do regarding a certain matter was troubling for me to accept. That's all I can say because it may all be garbage though my heart says different and I need to know again if Abraham Lincoln's original Assassination Chair was at Independence Hall between 1932 and 1939.

I apologize for the long response but I had no other way of presenting it.

Thanking you in advance.

Richard Ankony

****

Diethorn, Karie

To

Richard Ankony

CC

Renee Albertoli

Jun 5 at 1:47 PM

Mr. Ankony--

I see. Well, I'll check what records we have. Independence Hall was managed by the City of Philadelphia in the 1930s, and the records that survive of that management are spotty at best. Certainly, though, many historic things were displayed in Independence Hall at that time, including Civil War memorabilia. I think <u>it's very unlikely</u> that there were Lincoln documents among them, but I'll see what I can find out.

Regarding the chair that Lincoln sat in at Ford's Theater, this chair survives at the Henry Ford Museum in Dearborn. Henry Ford, the automobile magnate, purchased the chair at an auction in 1929. So<u>, I seriously doubt</u> that the Lincoln chair was ever in Independence Hall. But, again, I'll check. You can read about the chair at:

http://www.abrahamlincolnonline.org/lincoln/education/arocker.htm

I'll get back to you before the end of June with the results of my search.

Karie Diethorn

Chief Curator

Independence National Historical Park

National Park Service

US Department of the Interior

143 S. 3rd Street

Philadelphia PA 19106

phone 215-XXX-XXXX

fax 215-XXX-XXXX

cell 610-XXX-XXXX

****

To : Diethorn, Karie

Jun 5 at 3:05 PM

Thank you very much, I deeply appreciate your help and assistance.

Again Thank You in advance.

Richard Ankony

****

TO: Richard Ankony

Jun 5 at 3:07 PM

My pleasure.

Karie Diethorn

Chief Curator

Independence National Historical Park

National Park Service

US Department of the Interior

143 S. 3rd Street

Philadelphia PA 19106

phone 215-XXX-XXXX

fax 215-XXX-XXXX

cell 610-XXX-XXXX

****

Diethorn, Karie

To Richard Ankony   July 1, 2015
CC
Renee Albertoli

Mr. Ankony--

I find no record in our archive of either the Lincoln assassination chair or Lincoln written materials being displayed at Philadelphia's Independence Hall in the 1930s.

I do have an alternative suggestion though. Since the Lincoln assassination chair has been at the Henry Ford Museum in Dearborn MI since 1929 AND the Henry Ford Museum in Dearborn MI has a full size replica of Independence Hall (built in 1929), I think your father may be remembering a 1930s visit to the Henry Ford Museum's Independence Hall, rather than to the real Independence Hall here in Philadelphia.

I contacted the Henry Ford Museum, and the assassination chair's original wood frame is intact. So, regarding what your father remembers about "parts of the Assassination Chair...being taken", I think he saw people taking pieces of the chair's upholstery. While such actions are disturbing to us today, taking snippets of fabric from historic things as souvenirs was fairly common in earlier eras.

Regarding "certain original Abraham Lincoln papers being taken", I'm stumped. Henry Ford did collect some Lincoln material early in the 20th century. But, without a description of the contents of the material your father remembers, I can't comment on whether it's the same as the Lincoln material that the Henry Ford Museum owns today-- a single manuscript letter from Lincoln in 1859 discussing westward expansion of slavery.

I take it that the contents of the papers you're asking about were somehow controversial, specifically culturally offensive. If that relates to race, certainly Lincoln's views on slavery are well known. Early in his career, Lincoln wasn't an abolitionist, but he obviously became one during his presidency. Like his contemporaries, Lincoln could be considered "racist" by today's standards in that as a young man, he did not consider blacks and whites to be equal. I found no evidence that Henry Ford himself was overtly racist. However, Ford was most definitely anti-Semetic (he was extensively published on the subject). Lincoln, on the other hand, was not prejudiced against the Jewish people.

I hope this has been helpful.

****
Karie Diethorn
Chief Curator

Independence National Historical Park
National Park Service
US Department of the Interior
143 S. 3rd Street
Philadelphia PA 19106
phone 215-XXX-XXXX
fax 215-XXX-XXXX
cell 610-XXX-XXXX
****

TO: Mrs. Karie Diethorn   July 1, 2015
From: Richard Ankony

First thing I want to say is thank you very much for assisting me.
I think it was very considerate of you to take your valuable time and further look into this matter for my father and me.
I totally respect your professionalism and your opinion.

Regarding the alternative suggestion, my father and I have been to the Henry Ford Museum probably about a 100 times in our lifetime along with my whole family.
I have been there twice in the last month alone both inside and outside the museum.
As a patrol officer I used to patrol the grounds on many occasions so I am pretty familiar with the museum.
That said, my father has been at both locations (Independence Hall and the Henry Ford Museum) throughout his life and through numerous past and recent discussions with him he knows the difference between the two museums.

Nevertheless my father is very adamant on what he seen and what transpired around 1932, at Independence Hall, Philadelphia, Pennsylvania. For he has told me this same story numerous times since around 1990 or before that I recall.

That said based on my background every indicator I am receiving from my father tells me that he is telling the truth to the best of his knowledge and belief.

I should state my father has always been of clear mind and still is, despite hearing and visual setbacks now.

Regarding pieces of the original chair being taken, my father states in fact he did see pieces of the upholstery being taken and further states he sat in the chair along with his friends.

Regarding the original papers that were taken, though I am not an historian or a curator by no means, I found the contents of what my father was telling me within the original papers to be horrific. Again my father has stated over and over again to me that these original papers were taken at the same time that pieces were taken from the original Abraham Lincoln Assassination Chair.

I want to sincerely thank you again for your valuable assistance in this matter and I hope our avenue of communication will remain open despite the possible upcoming storm that has been brought to my doorstep.

Sincerely,
Richard Ankony,
July 1, 2015

****

To Richard
July 1, 2015   Today at 2:17 PM
Mr. Ankony--

Very well. If I run across any other pertinent information, I'll let you know.

****
Karie Diethorn
Chief Curator
Independence National Historical Park
National Park Service
US Department of the Interior
143 S. 3rd Street
Philadelphia PA 19106
phone 215-XXX-XXXX
fax 215-XXX-XXXX
cell 610-XXX-XXXX
****

Chapter 5 - The Lincoln Papers

During this same period of time when my father, Sammy and Mr. X, were at Independence Hall, Philadelphia, Pennsylvania around 1932 they made contact with the original assassination chair of Abraham Lincoln and also noticed original Abraham Lincoln papers that were on a table adjacent to "The Chair."

Both "The Chair" and "The Papers" were marked as original by placards placed next to the items in question at Independence Hall, Philadelphia, Pennsylvania.

After my father and his friends read the original Lincoln papers they were so moved by the contents which they found to be so out of character for Abraham Lincoln that Mr. X decided to take the three to five pages of the papers in question for himself.

According to my father regarding the contents of the papers, Abraham Lincoln had allegedly in place a "final solution" to the "black problem" which would have been implemented at the conclusion of the Civil War.

The papers apparently stated, according to my father, that Lincoln thought the blacks were, inferior, unsuitable and troublesome and wanted to send **all** the blacks back to Africa, Liverpool, England and London, England, after the Civil War ended.

Furthermore, according to my father, Abraham Lincoln was going to send both Southern Slaves and Northern free blacks to Africa, Liverpool, England and London, England.

Lincoln apparently intended to first free the blacks then deport all of them at the end of war, when in my sincere opinion divine providence interceded and did otherwise.

Lastly, Mr. X held the taken documents and later sold one during the depression for five dollars, which was considered a lot of money at that time.

Chapter 6 - The Interviews

<u>Interview July 19, **2012**</u>

<u>Note: The interview starts with a numbered question asked to my father and then his answered response. My father has a hearing problem and questions were repeated at times.</u>

Q1) Dad I wanted to ask you a question that you told me long time ago. You told me about you and your friends in Philadelphia where one of you grabbed a paper by Abraham Lincoln where he wanted to send the slaves back to Africa.

Ans: Yes. He did what again?

Q2) Do you remember that?

Ans: He did what again? I didn't get it ...something about Lincoln what was that again, go ahead Richard?

Q3) You went to Philadelphia you and your friends.

Ans: Yes.

Q4) You and Mr. X went?

Ans: Yah, me and Mr. X, at that time Mr. X wasn't married then and he met Little Meme, his wife, to be.

Q5) Okay, do you remember the year?

Ans: The year?

Q6) Yes?

Ans: Ahhh...Richard, it had to be in about 1938 (Note: Father born 1917)

Q7) 1938?

Ans: Yah, right around there.

Q8) Now didn't you tell me that there were papers there that Abraham Lincoln stated he wanted to send the slaves back.

Ans: Oh yes. Yes! Yes!

Q9) And Mr. X took the papers?

Ans: I think he did....he got that or got from others. At that time you could put your hands on the papers and I don't think Mr. X was the only one.

Q10) No?

Ans: There was some papers that he took there pertaining to Lincoln ....ahhh, pertaining to Lincoln in different ways and especially when he was shot.

Mr. X was one like yourself and I to a degree about history and that you know. It was nice to read these papers and see some of these different papers. Off hand, I am going to mark it down on paper and let you know more in detail.

Q11) Didn't you say about the papers how Lincoln wanted to send the slaves back?

Ans: Yes, yes...yes, he (Mr. X) had them and some other important papers. Like I said tonight I am going to put my mind to work and go back, because Mr. X and I would go on these trips where he met his wife to be, you know. It was nice...how we got started going there was....Mr. X's wife came from there?

Q12) That's Philadelphia?

Ans: Yes. Mr. X's wife was from there and Mr. X's wife was Russian and Alec's wife was Polish, and that's about it. And I am going to mark it down in detail and let you know. Anything more specific then that, that you wanted to know?

Q13) Yah, I wanted to know, what was the place you were in? Remember?

Ans: The place?

Q14) Was that where the Liberty Bell was?

Ans: Oh, ya, we went to...we touched the Bell, Richard.

Q15) Also, did they tell you the name of the book that Mr. X took the pages from? Do you remember?

Ans: Ahhh...it....was I think about a year before he got killed..shot, you know.

Q16) Okay, did you also say Mr. X took part of the seat he (Lincoln) was shot on?

Ans: Oh yes, yes, yes! He had a piece and I am sure he still got it. A piece of the chair, the cloth back of the chair where **the blood** from Lincoln was.

Q17) Okay...okay. So obviously Mr. X has it then?

Ans: I would say Richard, he sure kept it.

Q18) Okay...

Ans: Because this was the thing of the times whether they showed the law or whatever. They can understand, because it isn't like today, when everybody got their hands on stuff then. He (Mr. X) was interested in history like yourself and me too.

I think for a few years before Mr. X married that we had gone down there a few times because again like I say, reason being that ...ahh, Big Meme, Alec's wife, was from there, that's the reason.

We seen the Zeppelin (Hindenburg) explode. We were in Philadelphia just across the Delaware River where it exploded. It was coming to the moor where it anchored on. We had gotten there about a half hour later.

Interview ended regarding Lincoln Papers and Lincoln Chair.

Interview May 7, 2015

Q1) Who was Sam, what was his last name.

Ans: Sammy Hxxxxxn

Q2) Was there just Sammy, Mr. X and you there?

Ans. "Yes there was just Sammy, Mr. X and me"

Q3) Again did Mr. X take the papers?

Ans: Yes.

Q4) How many kids does Mr. X have if you remember.

Ans: Ahh...he has one that is a pilot.

Q5) What was his wife's name.

Ans: .....Ellen?

Q6) Did Mr. X take those papers?

Ans: Yes.

Q7) Did Mr. X ever state what he did what the papers?

Ans: After a while stuff like that disappears, where it exactly went I am trying to think. I am sure he had them or kept them or something.

Q8) Did he ever state he sold the papers or gave them to his kids?

50

Ans: I remember something came up about it but I don't know it completely...you know what I mean.

Q9) So you don't know exactly?

Ans: I know they were worth money, I know that. **They were the original stuff!**

Q10) They were the original stuff?

Ans: **Yes.**

Q11) They were the original papers?

Ans: **Yes, original papers**!

Q12) What were those original papers about? You mentioned it had something to do with the blacks in the past?

Ans: Something about having them sent back to Africa or something like that.

Q13) Again these were original papers?

Ans: Yes....yes! Lincoln said that! Lincoln said that!

Q14) He wanted to send them back to Africa?

ANS: He wanted to send them back. He figured, he foreseen, I think that was what the wording was, that they would be only trouble.

Q15) Is that right?

Ans: Yes.

Q16) Now again you seen the papers?

Ans: Yes, I seen them.

Q17) You seen those papers in Pennsylvania?

Ans: I seen them in Pennsylvania.

Q18) You told me in the past that you were with just Mr. X and Sammy?

Ans: Sammy was Mr. X's, brother-in-law.

Q19) After you seen those papers in that year in question did you ever see them again?

Ans: No, I think Mr. X tucked them away someplace Richard, but he didn't do anything openly with them.

He didn't go around saying look at what I got, he figured he's got a good thing.

I know that's how I would feel.

I got a good thing and he didn't go around showing it to people.

They wouldn't do anything to him because in those times people would take papers and odds and ends.

Q20) Did you ever hear who else may have seen those papers?

Ans: garbled

Q21) How many brothers and sisters did you have again?

Ans: Gladis, Katie, Gabriel, Elles, Alec..........Alec was my brother.

Q22) So, how many brothers and sisters did you have?

Ans: Nine.

Q23) When Mr. X took those papers, was it from a book, was it a diary or just open paper?

Ans: What they did in those days they shouldn't have never done. They didn't anticipate the future you know. Don't do this or this today because someone today will take the whole thing.

They were open papers, Richard.

Yes, anybody could take stuff then.

Yah, hell I seen the damn papers were original stuff they had different peoples names on them.

Q24) Do you remember how many pages were there? Was it a little or a lot or just a few?

Ans: Ahhh...moderate.

Q25) When you were in Philadelphia what was the occasion for being there?

Ans: Mr. X had met his wife there. A woman that was going to be his wife.

Q26) Were there any family members there also or just you three?

Ans: Me, Sammy and Mr. X and maybe just one more.

Q27) When Mr. X took those papers what was the particular reason why he took those papers?

Ans: In those days Richard when a person took this or that it wasn't consider bad then, as it is now.

Hell, people would go into Independence Hall place and take things and thought it was just an innocent thing.

Q28) How old were you at the time, do you remember?

(Note: Dad was born in 1917)

Ans: Ahhh....something like 18 years old. Something like that 17 or 18 years old.

(Note: My father told me in the past he was around 22 years old at the time and Mr. X was two to three years older then him. At this point in the interviews this event occurred according to my father around 1934 to 1939.)

Q29) Again Dad, the piece that was taken from the Lincoln chair where was it taken from?

Ans: Backside by the head.

Q30) Was there blood on it?

Ans: I think **there was a little** not a lot.

Interview ended.

Interview May 13, 2015

Q1) Regarding the Lincoln papers you seen was there anything different or unusual about them, for example was the color of the paper white?

Ans: Unusual?

Q1B) Yes, unusual?

Ans: No!

Q2) Dad, do you remember the year you were there?

Ans: I don't to tell you the truth.

Q3) How old were you, do you remember?

Ans: Well, I think I was around 18 years old.

Q4) Okay, you told me before you were 17 or 18 then you also said you were 22 years old. Which one do you think you were?

Ans: I am inclined to believe the lower one of 18 years old.

Q5) So you were with Mr. X and Sammy, just you three?

Ans: Yes.

Q6) Why were you there in Philadelphia?

Ans: There was a relative of ours from Philadelphia. (Apparently Big Meme and little Meme). Little Meme was Mr. X's wife and real nice, down to earth.

Q7) Do you remember anything Mr. X told you in regards to these papers?

Ans: Yes, some of the things that we had heard (seen?) was printed and we read about them later.

Q8) Wait, but yous had the papers?

Ans: Yes...yes!

Q9) So how did people find out if yous had the papers?

Ans: I don't know, I wonder sometime about that myself?

Q10) But if you read about it even though you had the papers, then someone knew?

Ans: I remember a lot of stuff was open where you could take some of the papers and stuff and tear the pages out and stuff like that. You could look and pick up the books and tear the pages out and stuff like that.

Why in the hell take the pages just take the whole damn book, at least the past would be intact for the future.

Q11) When you seen the papers dad, where were they?

Were they laying on the chair?

Were they next to the chair?

Where were they?

Ans: I think they were on the table.

Q12) And the table was next to the chair?

Ans: Yes, you would have liked to have seen that, Richard, this wasn't just a bunch of garbage, but you were looking at history.

You may not have realized it then, but later, you take into consideration the depth of what you seen. People in the future, not to far coming into the future, would think a lot about it.

We used to go there a lot, Richard, me and Mr. X. We went around Lakehurst, New Jersey where the Zeppelin was.

We seen those things, I remember I seen the Hindenburg go down.

Q13) You seen it go down?

Ans: Oh, ya! I was in Philadelphia, just across the Hudson (Delaware) River, it didn't take us long to get across. We seen it burning there. It was about 50% gone. It had static electricity and the gas (Hydrogen), the Germans tried to get that (Helium).

I seen people jump out of the cabin, not to high up.

I remember seeing a couple guys running back, we were about 175 feet (away) then.

Q14) You were 175 feet away from the Hindenburg?

Ans: Yes, I remember it hit the pylon and static electricity, somebody said somebody shot it, but I think it was static electricity. We were there a couple hours, at least, then you could go up to the whole damn thing.

Q15) In those papers that you said Mr. X took three to five pages what did Lincoln say that caught your attention?

Ans: Something about the blacks, something like that. They should be shipped back.

They came in by boat, commercial boat; they came in through the Philadelphia area that was a docking place at that time.

Q16) The papers stated Lincoln wanted to ship the blacks back, did he say where?
Ans: Back home.

Q17) Where would home be?

Ans: England. Well, the biggest place would be to Liverpool, England and London, England.

Q18) He wanted to send them to England?

Ans: Yah...yah

Q19) He wanted to send the blacks to Liverpool?

Ans: Yah...yah.

Q20) Why?

Ans: Because that's basically where the (boats) came from.

Q21) Did Abraham Lincoln want to send the blacks back to Africa?

Ans: That was the talk.Yah, there was talk about that. That wasn't a selfish thing but how people talked back then because that was the way people were. London and Liverpool were the two top places.

Q22) He also wanted to send them to Liverpool and London?

Ans: Yah...sure...sure!

Q23) Your saying Abraham Lincoln wanted to send the slaves here (in America) to Liverpool and London, England?

Ans: Yes..yes! They supposedly came from there.

The British, Richard, were the high fluting kind of people then.

The French were me, myself and I, taking care of their own self.

But the British wanted to get in on just about anything they could.

Q24) Your saying here that Abraham Lincoln wanted to send the slaves here to London, England and Liverpool England?

Ans: Yes! Yes!

Q25) That was in the papers?

Ans: Yah..yah. **I think Mr. X still got the papers too**! If I was still talking with him.

His wife (little Meme) didn't like Mr. X taking stuff here and there she was more down to earth.

Mr. X just didn't take it to just take it, he took it because he liked to collect stuff and stuff like that and in his mind he knew that in the future these articles or that would be worth something. I think he sold one page of some book and he got a pretty good price out of it.

Q26) So he sold a page?

Ans: Yah.

Q27) Of those pages he took, he sold a page?

Ans: Oh yah. Five bucks was a lot of money then...he didn't know....well that was a lot of money then. It would be like five hundred bucks today.

Q28) Did Lincoln say when he wanted to send the blacks back to Africa and England, did he say when he wanted to do that?

Ans: Lincoln, I think wanted to do that. **As soon as possible**, the way he talked at the time. Yah, take them and leave them. He had a lot of power then you know. We had the best of boats and the best of different stuff. And take those ships and go back and leave them off in England.

Q29) So he was going to leave them off in England too? Besides Africa?

Ans: Drop some of them to Africa. The British were the ones that brought most of them over. They didn't come by themselves.

Q30) Which of the blacks was he, Lincoln, going to send back, Dad? The southern blacks or all the blacks in America?

Ans: **All of them**! All of them now would not be what you think today in numbers. But if your talking several hundred that was a lot then.

Q31) Are you saying Dad, he wanted to send the slaves from the south and also the northern blacks back?

Did he say all the blacks as you said?

Ans: When the British came here and a lot of them (blacks) stayed on the eastern coast and with that .....what did they do?

Well most of the people (blacks) now you find, a lot..most of them, on the northeastern coast, you find that their names are just like the British.

Q32) Again Lincoln wanted to send all the blacks back?

Ans: Well the thinking then was, you thought, either they were inferior or something like that ..we couldn't make heads or tales with them, they never got along here and he said they would be better to just send them back and let them go back. With the war (going to be) over, they would cause a lot of problems then too.

Q33) So basically Abraham Lincoln freeing them was really to free them, to send them back?

Ans: Yes.

Q34) The freedom was to send them back and not to free them here? Send them back to Africa and England?

Ans: Something in that order? Lincoln was okay in himself. He had good ways and all that stuff but a lot of people didn't like him because he gave liberty here and liberty there and they figured they could make some money out of this (deporting blacks). People wanted to take the Africans and sell them. A lot of stuff broke down.

Q35) Was that in Independence Hall where you seen all this?

Ans: Yah, I never forgot it.

Interview ended.

<u>May 21, 2015 Interview.</u>

(Note: I am at the old age home showing my father pictures of the back of Lincoln's chair that were taken by my daughter, Tracy and my wife, Denise, most recently.

During this interview all the senior citizens were eating dinner and the large television was right next to us. My father wanted me to sit on his right side, which is his good ear, but I refused because it would put the television noise too close to the microphone.)

Q1) Dad, these pictures are the back of the Lincoln's chair, these (white spots) are the pieces that were taken? See the arrows pointing to the picture.

Do you remember which one Mr. X took?

Ans: Well, I think he took them both. He tore...he tore...

Note: According to my father he mentioned, at the time Mr. X took the first pieces of the chair from the back outer side none had been taken prior. So my father as he looked at the picture I showed him had a difficult time identifying where Mr. X must have taken all the pieces at that time.

My dad referred to the five or six missing pieces as "both", yet later in the interview, my father mentions that Mr. X was the <u>first</u> to take pieces of the Lincoln chair from the back outer side.

Days later I realized why my father had a difficult time identifying where exactly Mr. X took a 2" by 3" piece of fabric from the back outer side near the top of the chair.

For sure I thought a 2" by 3" piece of torn fabric from a chair would have been easy to identify.

Yet when I went back to the Henry Ford Museum and photographed the back outer side of the chair for myself with a high resolution camera, I realized the problem. The problem was when my father seen the initial pictures given to me by my daughter, her camera's flash showed up as white spots on the picture leading my father to believe they were the tear marks.

Yet when I took the high resolution photographs of the back outer side of the chair and enhanced them and studied them on my computer I could see there were basically just wear marks on the back outer side and not tear marks.

That is, there were no 2"x 3" tear marks on the outer back and upper side.

The conclusion I then reached was obviously these chairs, the one that my father swears to have seen around 1932 and what Henry Ford had since 1929 were not the same chairs or there was at this time more then one chair masquerading as original.

Otherwise this alleged "The Chair" at the Henry Ford Museum had been reupholstered to look like this deliberately to cover the 2"x3" tear or the second reason has a more sinister purpose which is to cover the replica and dress it like the original!

Or my father was duped with his friends at Independence Hall around 1932 and they themselves were dealing with a replica.

But Independence Hall was an established national archive museum for historical items for the United States of America and surely they wouldn't have put out a replica and claim it with "sign placards" as an original.

But Henry Ford's museum was opening up the same year Henry Ford got the alleged "The Chair" which was a million dollar tourist attraction and like all astute business minded men they are driven by money first, principles second.

Which begs the question, "Did Henry Ford get duped on the originality of the chair?

Or, with guilty knowledge did Henry Ford know, "a chair" if perceived by the public as "The Chair" and used as a tourist attraction at the Henry Ford's Museum was worth millions as a motive.

As my youngest daughter, Kelly, told me, "Up till now, Dad, it appears no one in the past until you has ever attempted to piece this all together."

(So at this time I want to present four word definitions.)

Original

definition:

: that from which a copy, reproduction, or translation is made.
: a work composed firsthand.
: made or produced first : not a copy, translation, etc.

Relic

definition:
: a survivor or remnant left after decay, disintegration, or disappearance.
: an object esteemed and venerated because of association with a saint or martyr.

Replica

definition:
: a copy in all exact details.
: an exact reproduction.

Fraud

definition:
: the crime of using dishonest methods to take something valuable from another person.
: a person who pretends to be what he or she is not in order to trick people.
: a copy of something that is meant to look like the real thing in order to trick people.

Q2) But which pieces do you think Mr. X took from...this one...this one...this one? This is the top of the chair? (pointing)

Ans: Well, I think he took a piece from the top.

Q3) Which piece would you say, he took if you can remember?

Ans: I think there were only two or three places where he clamped down. People in those days, at that time, I mean something like this comes along like this, everybody wanted a souvenir.

Who ever was in charge of (protecting) this stuff was a crackpot who should not have let anybody touch any of this stuff. But just the people who service this kind of material, you know.

Q4) These dots (in this picture) are tear marks as far that I know of, these here are light reflections from a camera?

Ans: Oh, I see.

Q5) So, he (Mr. X) either took that one or that one or took that one or these down here?

Ans: Yah, yah, yah, yah.......yah....yah, I remember touching that chair and everything.

You see that....well as time goes by people either get better or get worse and I think at that time they (the authority) trusted everybody like that.

You could touch stuff like that and you could go up and sit in the damn thing, like that.

That's not right, Richard. I mean, my God, all they want to do is say, "Oh, I sat in Lincoln's chair."

That don't make it right.

They got their rear end in the chair.....and that's it.

I remember the window (window encasement protecting chair) there (apparently Greenfield Village display) though now it is all covered and all guarded.

It's like gold for god sake and it is!

Lincoln, yah, Abraham Lincoln.

You know, there's a lot behind him if you read a little bit.

I read a little bit about him, but he was quite a man.

Q6) You don't remember the exact spot? Where the arrows I have?

Ans: What? That he took? I can't see them good. (Note: I then gave him my glasses.) I can see it like that.

All I can say he took from the top and several pieces were taken...before the dummies (authority) said we are going to take care of it. Now, take care of it in the beginning.

Q7) Okay, so you can't identify which one he took?

(Note: If there was only one, though my father is implying already that there were multiple pieces taken by Mr. X from the back of the chair.)

Ans: How many pieces was there?

Q8) It looks like there was about, one two, three, four, five, and here's one and this may be one, and this one and this one? Do you remember?

Ans: Well, **no**, well when I seen it, there was just one piece taken off (from the chair).

Q9) Oh, so there was none taken?

Ans: <u>There was just one piece taken</u>.

Q10) <u>Oh, so there was only one. So he took the first one, Mr. X?</u>

Ans: <u>Yah...evidently!</u>

Q11) So you cannot right now identify the piece that was taken except at that time Mr. X took the only one?

Ans: He took it.

Q12) Yah, Mr. X took the only one?

Ans: I would think so. <u>I didn't notice any torn or pieces or anything there then</u>.

Who ever was in charge, just imagine managing this kind of stuff and that's his job and all these things happen (tearing pieces from the chair).

Q13) In other words they were neglectful?

Ans: Oh, more then that.

I mean, if anybody is going to take your stuff, which is <u>only one of a kind</u>. That (assassination) chair is only one (of a kind). They didn't have any other thing there that I remember that Lincoln had (excluding the papers, or perhaps the desk).

Too bad, Greenfield Village I used to go with your mother so much, you know, to Greenfield Village, a lot. Yah...yah.

Q14) Well, okay, what I am going to do is, I am going to take more pictures of it (the chair) when I get there.

Ans: When you going?

Q15) Real soon, I am going to take high resolution pictures with a high resolution camera.

Ans: What's that do? Take more detail?

Q16) Yes, and when I do I will show it (the pictures) to you again.

Ans: Okay....that's really nice.

End of Lincoln Chair discussion.

<u>Interview June 07, 2015</u>

After receiving letter correspondence from the curator Karie Diethorn, Chief Curator, Independence National Historical Park, National Park Service, US Department of the Interior, with the promise to help in this matter, I decided one more time to interview my father to see and determine again if he still maintained his story.

I was convinced long ago my father was telling the truth and as redundant as it seems, I had to keep searching for inconsistencies or breaks in his story if any.

I felt there must be something I overlooked of what he has told me in the past since circa 1990 about the chair and the papers.

Yet again, I was surprised that my father didn't only maintain his story, he vehemently defended it, moreover he added more to it.

For as in the profession of polygraph examinations, you don't squeeze an innocent man until he pleads guilty. I was totally convinced as before that my father seen the original Abraham Lincoln chair and witnessed the pieces of upholstery taken and the original papers taken and I let the cards fall where they may.

Q1) Dad, I asked the curator (a real sweetie) at Independence Hall, that around 1932 to 1939, did Independence Hall have Abraham Lincoln's chair and Abraham Lincoln's original papers?

The curator stated she was going to help me.

Ans: Well she should make something out of it because the <u>people want to know the truth</u> because all that we knew about this particular article (chair) previously at the time or whatever was here, here and here.

<u>Hell now, they will try to back out of something like that.</u>

<u>They don't want to change their story because that wouldn't be good.</u>

<u>I hate to be in that kind of position....hell.</u>

<u>I mean all the people reading it (papers), Richard, and taking notes from it , I don't know, that would be a bad position to be in...hell.</u>

Q2) I told the curator, it was the original Chair that my father seen, right?

Ans: Yes.

Q2b)..... and it was the original Abraham Lincoln papers that you, Mr. X and Sammy seen.

Ans: Yes, what did she say about that?

Q2c) Well I told her that. That was the papers and that... that was the original chair. She then said basically the record is *spotty* at best but she would look into it. But then she came back stating something to the effect, she doesn't think the Abraham Lincoln papers were there.

Ans: Well she probably wasn't born then. You know some people talk about something of the past and their of the present themselves, their ideas don't come together with others you know. Too bad for them, hell.

Q3) I thanked her, for she didn't have to help me but she was a sweetheart this one. She stated she was going to look into it and come back in about a month (three weeks) and let you know about the Abraham Lincoln Chair and those Abraham Lincoln papers. Well, I am typing away on this paper because I am getting it ready.

Ans: Well, I am interested.

Q4) Dad let me ask you again, when you went to Independence Hall with Sammy and Mr. X, are you sure that was Abraham Lincoln's chair?

Ans: **According to what was written on it.**

4) Are you sure they were Abraham Lincoln's papers?

Ans: Well, Richard, as sure as I would know, for I have no authority to get into anything and **it was written this is this and that was that**.

I hate to see something that had been done and someone denying it and now approving it. Or trying to go from denial to approving.

In those days Richard they weren't trying to give a bad deal to the public.

Because if anybody found out about that then they are going to delve into who told you this and who told you that and yous are not sure of yourself.

5) Based on what you read that was the original chair at Independence Hall?

Ans: **Yes!**

5b) Based on what you seen on those papers those were the original papers?

Ans: **Yes!**

Note: My father's story hasn't broken from the beginning of the interviews nor since he told me the original story in 1990.

The reason why the redundancy in my questions is because I expect if this matter hits mainstream then "The Powers" will do everything possible to hide their shame for scamming the public by placing replicas instead of originals and deliberately duping an innocent unsuspecting public to milk their money.

Moreover, my experience in the past in investigations and interrogations is that some people or businesses will try to attack the "Whistleblower's" character in advance in order to cover their greed and shame.

Q6) Here's the problem, Dad? Henry Ford is apparently claiming that the chair didn't leave (The Henry Ford Museum) after 1929 or the Henry Ford Museum is claiming once they got the chair in 1929 it didn't leave and stayed at Greenfield Village. But three years later, down in Philadelphia, Pennsylvania you see the chair! Now how can that be?

Ans: Three years later?

Q7) Yes, maybe more, so what I am saying is....

Ans: One chair is there and the other there and their claiming it is the same chair? Well that can't be...you can't have that, someone will know!

Q8) The reason I have to keep asking this question Dad, as we go forward, is because I am writing a book on this. So are you sure you seen the original based on what you know...Abraham Lincoln's chair, your sure on that?

Ans: **Yes, cause, because it was written so! At that time!**

Q9) An as far as you know they were the original Abraham Lincoln papers?

Ans: **Yes, according to the way it was written and all that!**

Q10) Apparently, what happened Dad, Henry Ford got snookered, bamboozled, hoodwinked and duped and got the wrong chair. Independence Hall which is higher then Henry Ford Museum who apparently had the records and they don't know.

Ans: Well, hell if they don't have the records of important things, then who gives a damn!

Q11) To me as a police officer, the chain of evidence has been broken and it was broken back in 1929 and it would have never been discovered, until 1932, based on your story.

Ans: Yes.

Q12) ...and your story was that you seen it?

Ans: Yes

Q13) ..and if you seen it, the original chair, it cannot be at two different places at the same time?

Ans: Yes.

Q14) So one of them is a fraud?

Ans: Yes

Q15) Now Henry Ford is out here making money at $20 dollars a head now to come see the chair.

Ans: Your kidding?

Q16) He's making millions off this (replica) while your sitting in bed here and that's my findings.

Ans: Yes.

Q17) What I should be saying is that this chair, Abraham Lincoln got shot in, the government took the chair and then it went over to the Smithsonian Institute, then Henry Ford bought it.

But that isn't what happened, he bought "A Chair" and not "The Chair"!

Ans: He bought "A Chair" but not "The Chair"!

Q18) Because you seen "The Chair" at Independence Hall in 1932. And Independence Hall has right of way over Henry Ford; I mean it had (adopted and debated) the Constitution and Declaration of Independence there.

(Note: Isn't it strange that the Henry Ford Museum opens on October 21, 1929 and Henry Ford just happens to find a *National Treasure*, "A Chair" left abandoned and neglected after approximately 55 years of abuse just at the Smithsonian Institute warehouse and declares it "The Chair" and takes it up to his museum in 1929 as a tourist attraction? Then he throws the masses a grainy video with very little clarity and expects people to buy it as a continuing chain of evidence/custody claim.

Surprisingly the public bought it!

At this moment in the interview I was thinking of changing the name of this book too "Whose your Daddy?")

Q19) You know Dad, as you have already said *they know something is wrong* (that is, no adequate records, no chain of evidence/custody.) Because your testimony.......

Ans: Yes, you know it would be nice to cure it once (and for all) because if it keeps bouncing around like this the people or some people are going to say, what the hell?

I don't want anything to do with that if they can't make their minds up. I would like to know a fact is a fact and if so they state in the future. Is their going to be any reason for anybody in the near or distant future to change it?

Q20) Well that's what we are doing. You and me are going to change it.

For we are going to show that they don't know any better then we do!

Ans: Yes

NOTE: Make anyone who definitely states that Henry Ford 's Chair at the Henry Ford Greenfield Village is "Thee original chair" make them show the chain of evidence/custody of the chair, that is, the paper trail.

Then make them who defend the chair as original take a polygraph examination from a state licensed examiner to clear the matter at hand to prove what they read and know is totally true................and you'll have your answer!

Q21) They don't know if that (chair) is the original one or not?

Ans: Yes.

Q22) And my instincts tells me based on my experience that theirs is not the original. You saw the original. And I further think after you seen the original the damn thing was stolen!

Ans: Richard, that was at an early date when they wouldn't B.S. around, back then they had no reason for it. This was this and that's that.

Today their going to do it, then change records and I don't like that.

Once, Richard, people find out that records are being changed to pacify their beliefs or thoughts or anything like this, hell I wouldn't want to see a book or thing like that, it's crap, you know what I mean.

Because you say to yourself if I was younger, if I can't get it, right now, then I am not going to have my children read something only to find out later it is not so.

No, I wouldn't want that.

NOTE: This is why I decided to publish this book on the run and to make a second edition with corrections if need be, because my father feared or believed if we could show that the public was being deliberately taken advantage of then records could be changed or altered to fit the needs of the controlling powers.

But remember in any case Henry Ford has had "A Chair" on display since 1929 and at today's price of $20 to $45 dollars a head, that's a lot of money taken from the public under a false pretense if the chair is not original.

Q23) I agree, Dad. I wanted you to know that this (investigation) all came about by a mistake as you told me the story since about 1990, I remembered.

Ans: Yes.

Q24) And I happen to go with my wife, Denise, on April 15, 2015 to Greenfield Village to see the chair, Abraham Lincoln's chair and as I am looking at it I am thinking of you.

Ans: Yes.

Q25) Then I started thinking all these people (at the Henry Ford Museum) and all the money that is being made (about Abraham Lincoln) and all the stuff on television about this and that (celebrating Lincolns 150 year anniversary.)

Ans: Somebody is doing certain things to drive it into the peoples minds just for the buck.

Somebody is wrong there somewhere, has to be.

I would hate to be in that type of situation where somebody, like an older person says, I remember this and I remember that, now their trying to tell us different!

You wouldn't like it...you wouldn't like it.

Q26) You said it right, Dad.

No, you wouldn't like it because your seeing the replica and not the original and they are charging you money for the original.

Their lying to you!

Ans: No, I wouldn't like it.

You know, Richard, this (chair) is a fact going down in history and people want to know.

You can't take something and a few years later change it and change it and change it like that.

Like I told you all my information is true, I was of clear mind!

Q27) You know what's funny Dad, about all this, I think this is earth shaking.

But my wife, Denise, says, "Who cares?"

But it isn't that. It's about the truth!

It's about originality!

It's about replicas and people selling you a bill of goods that isn't so.

Here's the Lincoln chair, now give me $20 dollars but that isn't the chair."

Ans: Yes. Anybody writing a book would like clear knowledge on whose who.

You can't come back later and say it wasn't that way.

But you got to put it to the mind of the people that this was this and this was the way it was.

If your going to do that, my God, it's got to be the truth!

It's got to be the truth!

Q28) Now I got to ask you something, Dad, when you said Mr. X took pieces of the chair.

Ans: Yes, Mr. X did. Yes, fabric of the chair right around the neck (area).

Q29) (As I showed him a chair, I pointed to the outer back and upper side of the chair.) Right around here?

Ans: Yes, right in that area.

Q30) Was it on this side of the chair Dad?

Ans: Well, it was a covering and it was in one piece. And it was on the inside.

Q31) Was it this side? (As I pointed to the back outer side of the chair again.)

Ans: **Yes.** But they kept the padding (of the chair) on the inside. Yes right around that area. Towards the back. More of the back and maybe a little bit of the front.

Q32) So it was around the back outer side of the chair?

Ans: **Yes**, it came around there like that. Even Mr. X didn't think he should do it, (tear a piece of the Lincoln's chair fabric out) but it was really something. He shouldn't have done it but then somebody sooner or later would have done it and rip the whole damn chair out and everything.

Then several people would come forward saying, no that isn't the chair.

Then here we go again. But Mr. X got pieces from the real chair yet people will say no it isn't.

I remember those guys that worked on furniture in Philadelphia and they were furniture makers, you know. They were good, I used to watch them do it, (build chairs) I never forgot that.

Q33) (As I am pointing again to the outer back and upper side of the chair.)

So what your saying Dad, is the back outer chair off center towards Lincolns right shoulder about two inches, right in here?

Ans: Yes, sure. right. It wasn't a great big piece. It was a piece about like that. It wrapped around the front.

Q34) Oh? Show me how big again?

Ans: The piece of cloth? I would say, Richard, it would be like that. Here is the top of the chair. It came about like here in the back then it came down a little deeper in the front.

Q35) So it was dead center (on the outer back of the chair) **about two inches by two inches?**

Ans: **Yes, at least.**

On the width it was a little wider, Richard.

Just imagine someone coming up like that and just walking up and tearing a piece off.

But Mr. X did what a lot of people were doing too, you know, taking stuff like that, you know.

They didn't figure it was taking then.

You know I got this and show to mom or dad.

(At the time) I didn't think much about what Mr. X did, but I didn't think you should be doing that and let it be like that.

Q36) So basically (the tear on the outer back side of the chair) was about **three inches wide and two inches down, right near the center at the top of the wood?**

Ans: **Yes,** and the pieces taken off had not been cleaned and it had the **oily look like the oil they used in those days.** It had a change of color and you could see it between where the head was striking and where it was clear of it, you know. And there you could see from the front to the neck and where it came down to the neck you know. From what I understand I think his head and all that came too be slightly higher. Lincoln wasn't a short man.

Some stuff like this (original vs. replica), Richard, you want to have it settled because you won't have to come back to it all the time on what's what. People in the future are going to say, well hell, we read this article about information on this (chair) and this and now they are changing it 30 years, 40 years, 50 years later!

(Shaking his head) I don't know?

(Note: And that is precisely what is claimed about the original chair, that there was oil residue from people's hair on it.

Interview Ended.

Chapter 7 - Facts For and Against the Papers and Chair

Facts for Henry Ford's: "The Chair":

1) From the time Abraham Lincoln was murdered in 1865 to the time Henry Ford acquired the chair in 1929 was approximately 64 years.

"The Chair" Abraham Lincoln was shot in was immediately confiscated and held for evidence by the War Department. From there it goes to various places, put on display and finally arrives for the second time back at the Smithsonian Institute (1st-1869-1893, 2nd-1897-1928) for approximately 31 more years where it is again neglected, left abandoned and unprotected in a warehouse.

Some time later Harry Ford's widow of the Ford theater gets it back from the War Department.

It is then auctioned off for $2,400 dollars to Henry Ford in 1929.

2) Henry Ford takes the chair back to the opening/dedication of the Henry Ford Museum at Greenfield Village in <u>1929</u> for display where the chair has become the museums greatest tourist attraction.

3) To prove and maintain this chain of evidence/ chain of custody of the alleged "The Chair" Henry Ford shows a grainy and blurred video (<u>You Tube video: "Unpacking Lincoln's Chair 1929</u>") for public consumption.

This video shows a box being taken off a stagecoach containing some kind of object. The object in question appears to have been barricaded inside a box packed with filler where it is taken out of the box by jubilant workers who present an object that has the appearance of "a chair" and through some unknown process of transformation or osmosis it metamorphosizes itself into "The Chair."

4) In the article <u>"Three little known facts about the chair Abraham Lincoln was shot in"</u> on April 15, 2015 by Fox News, at Henry Ford Museum-Greenfield Village <u>regarding the chair's journey</u> .

The museum senior event planner, Jim Johnson, states that the "<u>unthinkable happened</u>" after the president died, "the chair began a <u>bizarre journey of misuse, damage,</u>

auction and relocation before it finally ended up at its permanent home, the Henry Ford Museum!"

Which apparently means, everything's in order, no problem here we got the original "We're good to go, cause Jim Bob put the identifier number right over here on the chair back in 1902 and perhaps again in1928!"

Even though "The Chair" was totally neglected and unprotected for 64 years and though my father sees another "The Chair" at Independence Hall in 1932, and an expert furniture craftsman hired by the federal agency per "The National Park Services" to build an "exact replica chair" sees another identical "The Chair" in the 1960's apparently at the Ford Theater which had been stated prior by the original owner of "The Chair" in 1865 that "The Chair" was part of a set and suite we therefore are suppose to believe the Henry Ford Museum has the original!

This is based solely on the assumption that only one of these type chairs was made despite the fact that at least five (5) chairs are already floating around the country that is known.

I am unaware of one type of chair model being made just one time, but rather hundreds if not thousands of the same type of chair model is made commercially.

Mr. Henry Ford just happened to acquire the original "The Chair" and put it in place at the Henry Ford Museum in 1929 precisely at the exact time his Greenfield Village Museum was opening which was bought for pennies on the dollar at an auction over other bidders and purchased from a widow who didn't know who had "The Chair" or where it was, and we are supposed to buy that story?

Nothing suspicious here folks....move along!

The video film proves it to the public.......really?

5) The national curator from Independence Hall first states, even though the records were "spotty at best of those that survived in 1930's from Independence Hall" followed by "I find no record in our archive of either the Lincoln assassination chair or Lincoln written materials being displayed at Philadelphia's Independence Hall in the 1930s" implies politely that my father's event never happened, or it's a figment of his imagination or there are other unknown celestial mechanics involved here, yet to be discovered.

Furthermore because there are no records of the chair or the papers at Independence Hall during my father's visit and even though records were "spotty at best of those that survived" this therefore must imply that the Henry Ford Museum has the original?

6) Henry Ford says it's so, what more proof do you need?

7) It is what it is!

8) The Henry Ford Museum claim by telling the national curator of Independence Hall they have "the assassination chair's original wood frame intact."

This means with 100% certainty "the frame" or just parts of it is the original assassination chair of Abraham Lincoln, which apparently means the unique identifier given to the alleged "The Chair" in 1902 by the Smithsonian Institute is what the Henry Ford Museum claim is primarily or solely based on? Even though a unique identifier could have been duplicated in 1928 and placed on a duplicate chair, replica chair or relic chair and sold at the auction.

Now those are the known facts for Mr. Henry Ford and his "The Chair!"

Facts for Henry Ford "The Papers":

1) The national curator at Independence Hall stated in regards to my father's visit around 1932 to the effects, "It's very unlikely that there were Lincoln documents among them" which highly implies my father was mistaken again.

2) Further the records held and maintained by the city of Philadelphia around 1932 were "spotty records at best of those that survived" must imply that the papers were never there?

In my police definition the word "spotty" in this context means, "a non consistent and sporadic pattern of maintaining records", "unknown", "ain't sure", "a 25% probability", "Don't know whose your daddy?" and "Ahh..let me get back with you, it's happy hour" or "WTF cares?"

3) The national curator from independence Hall states, "I find no record in our archive of either the Lincoln assassination chair or Lincoln written materials being displayed at Philadelphia's Independence Hall in the 1930s."

Yet despite that statement "no record of the papers and chair being there at Independence Hall" which was drawn from "records that survived or were spotty at best" subtly implies that my fathers experience and witnessing to this critical event involving one of Americas most cherished **National Treasure** did not happen.

"That's the proof and I am suppose to buy that?"

Not this American, for I may have been born during the day, but not yesterday!

Facts for my father: "The Chair" and "The Papers":

1) There is no definitive chain of evidence/chain of custody for the chair or the papers. The chair in essence was abandoned, mutilated, mistreated, neglected as if an "orphan" since the moment of Abraham Lincoln's assassination.

The same goes for the Lincoln papers that were unknown and went unprotected which invited misappropriation of the goods.

1B)The only plausible reason for this **National Treasure,** "The Chair" to be so horribly neglected and mistreated at the Smithsonian Institute must be that it was perceived as a replica taken from somewhere and placed as the original " The Chair."

Yet in my opinion, the original "The Chair" at some point(s) in time was stolen, destroyed or lost and is still out there.

2) Why would Mr. X take pieces of upholstery and one as large as (2"x 3") from a replica chair, which would be meaningless?

3) Why would Mr. X take Lincoln's papers if they were not original and meaningless?

4) Why would a buyer, buy one of Lincoln's paper from Mr. X if not original?

5) Why after reading the paper's contents and realizing the importance and monetary worth would Mr. X take a replica and place himself in harms way then exit the premise of Independence Hall with it?

Why would my father be so fearful all these years of telling the story of the papers and the chair that occurred around 1932 if the fabric taken from Lincoln's chair along with papers taken from the adjacent desk were duplicates or replicas?

6) The question that the national curator presented that perhaps my father was mistaken on the location of the chair and the papers, yet my father told me specifically he has never been to the Smithsonian Institute or the Henry Ford Museum with Sammy or Mr. X together but only at Independence Hall, Philadelphia, Pennsylvania, with them.

Moreover, Sammy was from Philadelphia and his sister which Mr. X was going to marry was also from Philadelphia which was the reason why they were there.

This means that the national curator of Independence Hall who innocently implies that my father probably mistaken his location of his witnessed event therefore is unfounded.

7) My father never changed his story for at least 25 years. Which is extremely important in the field of investigation whether it be in police work, investigative work or in the polygraph field.

For a consistent story is indicative of truthfulness. It is not totally conclusive yet it is a very strong indicator for truthfulness.

8) My father is an honest man. This I know firsthand and at point-blank range for 68 years of my life so why should he lie about this matter when no leverage or advantage can be gained?

While Mr. Henry Ford was a very successful business and famous man, yet his ways and means that he acquired his fortune and fame doesn't necessarily imply morals and ethics was placed at the forefront of his endeavors.

9) My father has nothing to gain by stating the same story for 25 or more years. There would be no reason for my father to tell this story if it was a lie let alone to his family. My father was not egotistical or arrogant or drunk with power but rather just a simple selfless individual who loved his wife and children and took care of them. My father always put his family first before money...always!

Could I say the same about Mr. Henry Ford? I won't dare answer that though "the streets are talking" so I prefer to leave that answer to the expert historians.

10) Even now my father is sane with clear mind! Yes, even now at 98 years old my father is still my hero and can tell many stories of yesteryear with uncanny accuracy in precise detail of which one story is the Lincoln chair and his papers.

11) The Abraham Lincoln assassination chair sits neglected as a piece of junk, figuratively speaking in human terms, "The Chair" has become an "orphan".

It was unwanted, unkempt, mistreated, neglected, abused, forgotten and mutilated. So much so, in 1928 when Blanche Chapman Ford, the widow of Harry Ford who was the original owner of "The Chair" from the Ford Theater did not know where "The Chair" was and further asked these startling questions to the Smithsonian curator "**Is it true that you have the chair**?", and, "**If so, will you kindly tell me why it is not on display?**"

Imagine a million dollar baby and the owner does not know where it's at?

Which begged the second question **"Why it is not on display?"**

In my opinion "The fix was in" and the curator of the Smithsonian Institute, who just got "Called out" didn't have a damn clue where that abandoned chair was and that's why it wasn't on display!

Upon being "called out" the curator at the Smithsonian Institute probably found another identical chair and put the same identifier on it and "gave up the ghost" to Blanche Chapman Ford!

Henry Ford doesn't give a damn whether the chair is original or not as long as the public perceives it as original and pays 20 dollars to 45 dollars a head at current prices.

Henry Ford buys the chair on the cheap among other bidders but $2,400 is a hedge bet incase the scheme falls through. That is, the original chair cost a lot of money but a duplicate chair cost just a little money so a cheap low bid could imply buying a duplicate.

To further mislead and throw investigators off the trail, Henry Ford presents to the public a grainy video as a contrived and continued chain of evidence/chain of custody which is bought hook line and sinker by the public and therein lies the lesson.

"Stupid is, as Stupid does!

12) For the curator of the Smithsonian Institute to claim "The Chair" was not put on display because basically it was too violent for public consumption is pure bull. For the chair had already been put on display and apparently people were so frightened of it, that they sat on it, relaxed on it and allegedly laid their curly locks of greasy hair on the same spot where Lincoln's brains were once, which doesn't make sense.

13) "The Chair" was not put on display because it could not be located and in order <u>to prevent a national embarrassment</u> the curator of the Smithsonian Institute had to in my opinion found a duplicate chair and placed the same identifier on it and handed it over to Blanche Chapman Ford.

14) Blanche Chapman Ford now in possession of the alleged "The Chair" sells it for $2,400 dollars on the cheap when she had to know <u>it was worth millions</u> at an auction where I perceive numerous other bidders were present and like Henry Ford all realized the potential worth of the chair.

Why, would Blanche Chapman Ford sell a million dollar baby so cheap?

Well, my take is this because <u>neither the other bidders, Henry Ford or Blanche Chapman Ford knew in fact for sure if the chair being auctioned was the original or a replica</u>.

<u>They didn't know for sure what they had!</u>

This would support the theory why it was sold and purchased cheaply!

15) Remember again, to Henry Ford it was irrelevant if the chair was original.

The curator at the Smithsonian Institute had to tell Blanche Chapman Ford that what he gave her was original. What else could he say, "I don't know where this **National Treasure** is at?"

Blanche Chapman Ford, apparently was not totally convinced 100% she had the original in her possession yet she realizes that a possible duplicate or replica in her possession would not draw money, so in my opinion she claims it's original **but** sells low to unload it.

Henry Ford, a cunning businessman with a new museum opening needs a "prime attraction" to draw in millions of dollars because the public needs to see more then junk cars or rusty farm tools on display because at that time they were still being used by the public.

So Henry Ford, plays the game, buys the chair for $2,400 and confirms its authenticity by showing a movie about an object being unboxed at the Henry Ford museum.

The bubbling starry eyed public look upon this chair with glee as if it was a unearthed sarcophagus from the pharaohs of Egypt.

This implies millions of dollars of ongoing revenue and a possible flimflam or possible fraud until now, when 85 years later my 98 year old father comes along and says, "My son, the original chair cannot be at two places at the same time. Make it right Richard, show the people the truth."

Where I relied, "So let it be written, so let it be done!"

16) The historians say they found spots of blood on Lincolns chair but of whose is unknown, yet my father states the 2"x 3" piece taken from the back outer side of the chair had blood on it which was a totally different location from the hair oil on the back inner side.

My father stated it was "a thumb size blood stain" on the patch taken and possibly surrounding area. Furthermore, the blood was visually recognized by its brown color which was totally different from the surrounding fabric of the chair.

This would imply at least two different chairs had to be in circulation. Moreover a gunshot wound to the head as in suicides or murders of which I have witnessed numerous times in 25 years of police work leaves blood everywhere!

This would imply that my father witnessed the original chair for he and his friends did recognize blood on the outer back and upper side of the chair and that it was different in color from any alleged hair oil on the inner back upper side.

17) Henry Ford's Lincoln chair on display at the Greenfield Village, as I witnessed, does not have the 2' x 3" piece of upholstery missing as my father witnessed taken in 1932 from the outer back and upper side of the chair.

This would imply either two different chairs or chair alteration for legitimate or illegitimate purposes.

18) The U.S. government admitted pieces of the chair was missing, clipped and "mutilated" within days after the assassination in1865 yet except for the left arm of the chair at the Henry Ford Museum, of which I just observed in July 2015, the chair shows primarily wear marks. This would imply it may not be "The Chair" and/or it was reupholstered to cover up a replica.

19) Henry Ford stated he had the original chair in 1929 and it was not sent to Independence Hall thereafter. Yet my father and friends made contact with the original

chair and papers in 1932 as <u>stated by placards adjacent to the chair</u> at Independence Hall, Philadelphia, Pennsylvania.

Why would Independence Hall curators lie or mislead the public when they are a national and highly respected museum?

This would confirm again that there were multiple chairs of the Lincoln rocking chair circulating.

I mean how hard would it be for a master furniture craftsmen to make a duplicate Lincoln assassination chair in secret?

Based on what my father told me, he witnessed these furniture craftsman at work in Philadelphia and that they were very good at their profession. So it seems a duplicate chair could have easily been made especially when millions of dollars of revenues from tourists could be drawn just from it's presence.

20) When I showed my father a picture of the back outer side of Abraham Lincoln's assassination chair to identify the exact spot where Mr. X took the 2"x 3" piece of fabric he could not readily recognize the spot from the picture because the torn pieces were not there that he witnessed in 1932 which implies the chair has been altered or there are other similar chairs in circulation.

21) The chair has been upholstered for one of two reasons, one to dress it up or two to cover their trail of a duplicate, replica, relic or a partial original chair which is probably the reason why the Henry Ford Museum refused the government and their expert furniture craftsman access.

22) Henry Ford showed a 1929 "grainy" video where it is stated as an "object" by the Detroit Free Press journalist instead of "a chair" that was taken from the box which to me further corroborates my observation and opinion of the video that the chair was not readily identifiable.

23) Where's the legal and professional paper trail and the credible chain of evidence/chain of custody to show undeniably that this *National Treasure* is in fact Lincoln's chair?

Why isn't the facts known to the public up front, for they have the right to know the truth?

Why all the hush-hush and secrecy of the chair as if above "Top Secret?" Which would imply to me that someone is hiding something from the public's eye for a good reason and the best reason I can think of is money.

Moreover if there is no valid and legal paper trail presented to the public to openly review, then the chairs authenticity must remain in question beyond a reasonable doubt and until proven otherwise it cannot be declared as an original!

Being the devil's advocate, in my opinion, **nobody** knows the true story of the chair and for any institution or museum to claim with 100% certainty that the chair they possess is in fact "The Chair" is totally misleading to the public when at best maybe only the frame may be original, if that, which is doubtful.

Again why all the secrecy and denial of investigation of the chair?

Why?

Well, one important reason is when a federal agency like "The National Park Service" hires an <u>expert furniture craftsman</u> to duplicate Abraham Lincoln's assassination chair for the Ford Theater Museum, in Washington D.C and is <u>denied</u> access to the alleged original at the Henry Ford Museum <u>strongly suggest somebody is hiding something</u>.

Now remember Henry Ford has made billions of dollars from the United States Government over the years and throughout the World Wars where a lot of American blood has been shed on the field of valor to uphold his institution and his freedom.

Yet when the United States Government asks Henry Ford's Greenfield Village if they can take measurements or get specifications of their perceived **National Treasure** "The Chair" that they are holding and flaunting as an American treasure for 85 years of which is bringing in millions of dollars in revenue from the American people.....**THEY REFUSE!**

Henry Ford's Museum **refuses** access to the chair and denies the Ford Theater, the expert furniture craftsman and the United States Government request to further honor and show respect for this great president in question by <u>allowing them to take just measurements of the frame.</u>

Why?

When I asked this question to professionals, their spontaneous utterance was identical to mine.

The reason or speculation was that Henry Ford's Museum was not concerned or afraid of the National Park Service, nor the Ford Theater but rather their concern and dreadful fear was what this southern expert furniture craftsman would detect **something about the frame that is being claimed as original was in fact not.**

There was something about the chair's frame that only an expert furniture craftsmen could see, detect and recognize as original from a replica to a relic to a fraud that somebody did not want him to see.

Furthermore this expert furniture craftsman was southern to boot and wouldn't for one iota hesitate to tell the truth.

This is in part why I believe why Henry Ford refused access to it!

24) My father who sat in the chair still could not positively recollect if there was or was not hair oil on the back inner side of the chair. If there wasn't this would imply a second chair.

25) Probably among the highest curators in the country, the chief curator at Independence Hall stated that "Independence Hall was managed by the city of Philadelphia in the 1930's, and the records **that survived** of that management is **"spotty" at best."** Which implies that there were no accurate record keeping systems in place at that time around 1932.

Which further implies if such a distinguished museum as Independence Hall has "spotty records at best of those that survived" during that time then *what would that imply about less distinguished museums and those going back to 1865 at the time of Lincoln's assassination*? This should strongly imply that there was no definitive record keeping anywhere.

26) Henry Ford claims he purchased the original chair in 1929 at an auction, yet my father after 25 years of telling me the same story failed to break his consistency which is a strong indicator that is indicative of truthfulness.

27) Henry Ford buys the chair at an auction for $2,400 in 1929 which obviously means other wealthy bidders were present. The others must have known a chair of this

nature would draw a huge tourist crowd over time in addition to being prestigious to have, yet Henry is able to secure it and buys it "on the cheap."

An original should have gone for a lot more money then $2,400, unless of course it's originality must have been in question and no one but Henry would take the chance on getting caught with a possible duplicate like this.

Henry Ford knew the purchase of the chair was worth the risk, whether a duplicate or original, for on one hand he loses a measly $2,400 dollars if the chair is discovered as a duplicate but on the other hand, if no one is the wiser and the chair is perceived as original, it could be worth possible millions as an income for his new museum as a primary tourist attraction, which it was. The best way to cover his tracks going forward after the purchase of the chair would be to show to the public an indistinguishable video which he did.

28) How could my father for 25 years remember everything in vivid detail of the location of the Lincoln papers that was adjacent to the chair and it's shocking contents if it wasn't original? Though I am not an historian yet as best as I can tell what my father read is unknown. to historians and the public in general.

How could my father have read and seen Mr. X take those Lincoln's papers along with the upholstery piece that was torn off from a specific location from the back outer side of the chair if it wasn't an original?

The Smithsonian Institute nor the Henry Ford Museum has ever had this type of setup of "The Chair," with an adjacent table containing original Lincoln papers on open display to the public.

Further my father told me he has never been to the Smithsonian Institute in his life.

Furthermore, the Henry Ford Museum has never admitted that they had this type of setup (chair, table, and papers together) in the last 85 years.

Plus my father has told me he has never been to the Henry Ford Museum with Sammy and Mr. X.

This implies that my father was witnessed to a real authentic event and what he is claiming to be true is to the best of his knowledge and belief.

29) My father has nothing to gain by lying, but Mr. Henry Ford has millions to gain by lying.

30) Henry Ford Museum is now a world wide tourist attraction and at $20 to $45 a head has millions to gain by claiming their main attraction "The Chair" is original.

31) Henry Ford Museum stated the chair never left the museum since 1929, except for Grand Rapids, Michigan, yet my father sees it with friends in 1932 in Philadelphia. Again this implies multiple chairs or someone got duped big time.

32) Based on what's known to *the best of my ability* as a non-historian, I believe that the chair's present existing chain of evidence/chain of custody, if looked upon as proof of a crime during trial would have been thrown out by every judge in the country.

33) Henry Ford was driven by money not honesty.

34) Henry Ford had much to gain monetarily if this chair was the original or a replica. It was a no lose situation as long as the public believed his golden fleece.

35) My father stakes his reputation on his testimony and would gladly take a polygraph if he could.

36) I seriously doubt that any historian who maintains the premise that at the Henry Ford Museum at Greenfield Village, there sits "The Chair" that is, the original chair that Abraham Lincoln was assassinated in would offer themselves to be polygraphed regarding their claim.

37) So I am "calling out any historians", if they maintain the premise that they absolutely know with 100% certainty that the Lincoln Chair at the Henry Ford Museum since 1929 is the original "The Chair" in it's entirety that Abraham Lincoln was assassinated in on April 14, 1865.

I mean the whole chair as claimed and not part of it!

Further, if they do believe it show proof why and then allow that proof to be inspected by neutral parties.

My offer is this to defenders of the Henry Ford Museum's, Lincoln's chair. Take the polygraph examination or admit that you don't know with absolute certainty (100%) that the chair at the Henry Ford Museum is the original Abraham Lincoln's chair or the original Abraham Lincoln chair in it's entirety.

38) The contents of the papers drove my father and his two friends to take three to five pieces of original Lincoln papers. There was something they read that was so alarming they decided to take the papers at risk. Why do this for a replica?

39) My father stated that one of the original Abraham Lincoln papers was sold during the depression for five dollars, so no doubt who ever bought it also believed in it's importance and originality.

40) According to the Henry Ford Museum brochure the rocker "languished in storage for decades." Which means neglected, uncared for, fade away as in disappear or put out of sight, or slipped out the back door to street hustlers or to a wealthy merchant.

So if this *National Treasure* was so neglected for 64 years until Henry Ford purchased it in 1929 at an auction and its significance and monetary worth was known from the very beginning since the time of the assassination, it is not far fetched to conclude that the original chair could have been misappropriated at any time during these 64 years.

41) In an article dated April 16, 2015, Three little known facts about the chair Abraham Lincoln was shot in, Henry Ford Museum, senior events planner, Jim Johnson, stated, "We kind of have the bookends on Lincoln's career." Johnson then states, "the chair began a bizarre journey of storage, misuse, damage, auction and relocation before it finally ended at its permanent home. From what we understand, people who worked at the Smithsonian probably, custodians or people like that, used it as a kind of break area."

Mr. Johnson stated that this likely happened around the end of the 19th century and that they (workers, et al) sat in the chair, got lots of grease on it and might have even taken off pieces of the chair. "

He further goes on to say, "the black walnut chair was part of a set or suite."
A bizarre journey?

You bet it was bizarre, the chair started somewhere and it is still out there!

The chair was used as a break area, misused, damaged and abandoned allowing the possibility to be either stolen or trashed.

What does part of a set or suite mean?

Does that mean more then one, it sure sounds like it to me?

The Henry Ford Museum never stated, as far as I know, that just "The Chair" was the only one of it's type and model built. Therefore, by default it leaves the belief that there could have been hundreds of these chairs built!

42) My father stated many times, "Who wants to see a replica?"

Which implies if what he seen at Independence Hall was a replica he wouldn't have wasted his time to tell me about it.

43) My father further stated when he did see the Abraham Lincoln chair and papers at Independence Hall, it was identified with placards, saying that they were original. Furthermore, I believe Independence Hall would be less likely to lie about the authenticity of their exhibits because of their national prominence as compared to the Henry Ford Museum.

44) My father after witnessing Henry Ford's intentions at the "Battle of the Overpass" when the Ford goons attacked and beat honest working men felt Henry Ford was strictly driven by money and "The Chair" or "A Chair" was a money maker for his museum!

That is, it's about money.

45) Seeing that the original Lincoln assassination chair is indeed a **National Treasure,** "We the People" should know the truth with absolute certainty on the authenticity or percentage of originality of the chair at the Henry Ford Museum.

Therefore, a polygraph examination is in order and should be administered regarding the originality of the Henry Ford perceived Lincoln assassination chair.

Moreover any hidden proofs regarding the chair's originality should be made available to the public to openly scrutinize upon request.

Polygraph examinations should be administered and the results stated publicly on the record whether the defenders of the chair passed or failed including any admissions that the historians stated regarding the chairs uncertainty.

The questions on the polygraph examination to be asked the historians who claim with absolute certainty that their chair is original should be along these lines, which is followed by their respected answer:

A) Are you 100% certain that the Abraham Lincoln's assassination chair at Greenfield Village is the original chair that Abraham Lincoln was assassinated in, in it's entirety? (Yes or No)

B) Are you 100% certain that the Abraham Lincoln assassination chair was never at Independence Hall, Philadelphia, Pennsylvania between 1932 and 1939? (Yes or NO)

C) Do you know absolutely 100%, the chain of evidence/chain of custody where Abraham Lincoln's assassination chair was and the names of it's overseers since the date of his assassination until now? (YES or NO)

D) Do you know if the Abraham Lincoln's assassination chair claimed presently at the Henry Ford Museum is a replica, relic or a fake in any way? (Yes or No)

E) Do you believe 100% that the original Abraham Lincoln chair could not have been stolen sometime in the past and replaced by a replica? (Yes or No)

F) Is it possible that the Abraham Lincoln's chair now presented at the Henry Ford Museum is not the original chair Lincoln was assassinated in? (Yes or No)

G) Do you have any guilty knowledge or are you part of a known conspiracy to defraud the American people by claiming the Abraham Lincoln assassination chair presently held at the Henry Ford Museum is a fraud in part or in whole? (Yes or No)

If they laugh at this idea to take a polygraph examination and refuse to take the examination then they are laughing at _us_, **"We the People"** which will convince me nearly 100% that the chain of evidence has been broken long ago and as I suspected the Henry Ford Museum is peddling "A chair" and not "The Chair" which would negate the originality and claim of the authenticity of their Lincoln chair in question which would most probably constitute a fraud and this matter forwarded upwards to higher authorities.

46) In a letter, the owner of the chair, Blanche Chapman Ford, further asks the question to the Smithsonian Institute curator, Theodore Belote, if he has the chair, "If so, will you kindly tell me why it is not on display?"

The response was a lame answer that the chair was too horrible to display considering the circumstances.

Which implies to me the curator covered himself and most probably did not know where the damn chair was because it was neglected, abandoned and forgotten for many years.

47) In 1902, the alleged "The Chair" was finally given <u>after 37 years</u>, a unique "Accession number-38912 and was catalogued in the Department of Anthropology."

This number is a unique number given to each new acquisition as it is entered in the catalog of a library or museum.

This begs the question, "Why in God's name did this alleged "The Chair" a **National Treasure** take 37 years to receive a unique identifier number, so it could be identified?"

Why did they have to identify something supposedly so easy to recognize as the original or was it because they had concerns that there were "others" out there?

Am I to assume that the Smithsonian Institute did not identify its exhibits until 1902 though it was established in 1846 "for the increase and diffusion of knowledge?

What I see is "A Chair" was identified and tagged but due to the gross abandonment and neglect throughout the years "The Chair's" originality could not be determined with absolute certainty now.

Which further begs the question, "Could this "Accession number-38912 be duplicated again and put on a duplicate chair?"

Further, prior to being given this number for the chair in 1902 what was the positive identifier used before it was given the identifier for the last 37 years?

If any?

Could Henry Ford who makes cars and puts VIN numbers on newly made cars also do this for the chair?

It should be obvious by now that there are hundreds of ways of beating the system when records were "spotty at best of those that survived" coupled with greed.

In my opinion without a presentation of positive and compelling evidence that would stand the scrutiny of a judge and jury in the public square and when one considers the known evidence available about the chair should lead any reasonable and prudent person to suspect a scam.

48) The national curator from Independence Hall also stated in her last message that the Henry Ford Museum states, "the assassination chair's original wood frame is intact."

So that tells me what now, only the wood frame is original and everything else is not? Then is it still an original or a replica?

That said, I have to assume that the wood frames originality is based solely on it's "Accession number-38912 which must be somewhere on the frame. Though I took numerous photographs of the chair I could not visually locate the identifier that was given to it in 1902, 37 years after the assassination of Abraham Lincoln.

So giving benefit of the doubt I am going to assume the identifier was placed beneath the chair or in some discreet location on it.

Otherwise, should I walk by faith that it's there?

What if it's not there?

So Henry Ford is home free with "a chair" perceived as "The Chair", until 1932 when my father walked into Independence Hall, Philadelphia, Pennsylvania and with friends see signs and placards stating that before them is the original Abraham Lincoln's chair and adjacent to the chair are original Abraham Lincoln papers.

They sit in the chair, pieces of upholstery are taken especially a 2"x 3" piece from the back outer side of the chair with blood on it, not hair oil, and also take three to five pages of Lincolns original papers stating his "**final solution**" in regards to "**the black problem.**"

49) It was stated by the national curator at Independence Hall that there is no record of Abraham Lincoln's assassination chair ever being at Independence Hall.

Though my father is in 100% disagreement in regards to the curator's statement which is based on her research from records maintained at that time by the city of Philadelphia, "of those that survived", were "spotty at best".

However if Abraham Lincoln's deceased body was laid out there in Independence Hall shortly after his assassination for all the citizens of Philadelphia to mourn and pay their final respect too, then it stands to reason that Independence Hall was considered to be a primary national exhibit and museum.

This implies that if the president's body was found fitting to be laid out at Independence Hall which must have been considered a sacred place then obviously his chair that he was shot in would also be considered to be worthy to be exhibit at that location also.

That being said, in no way does the incomplete records maintained by the city of Philadelphia during the time my father visited Independence Hall rule out the possibility that Abraham Lincoln's assassination chair was there.

Remember, in 1865 Abraham Lincoln's assassination chair was taken from "a suite "or set of chairs."

This would imply that at the time of Lincoln's assassination there may have already been more then one chair of this type in circulation.

Furthermore, the chair Abraham Lincoln was assassinated on as far as I know was not the "one and only" chair of this type made. This chair was taken from the quarters of Harry Ford so that chair's model most probably was made numerous times and was in circulation at that time.

Moreover, in 1932 my father stated that he and his friends seen the original chair at Independence Hall which would imply at that time there was at least three chairs in circulation.

But the "coup de grace" or death blow came when the United States government, the Department of Natural Resources, in the 1960's <u>asks</u> the Henry Ford Museum to see the chair which is claimed to be the original so that an expert furniture craftsman could measure dimensions of the chair in order to build a replica to exact specifications for the Ford Theater. But to their surprise **the Henry Ford Museum denies them access**!

Henry Ford who has made billions of dollars off the sweat, blood and tears of the American people through multiple wars when asked by a federal agency for assistance in upholding Lincoln's legacy suddenly disenfranchises itself from American history and it's people.

Why?

Why, would the Henry Ford's Museum deny the American people this right to see the chair up close or be allowed to measure it or study it and finally to authenticate it if need be?

Was it for money or perhaps it was something that an expert furniture craftsman <u>might discover and reveal</u>?

Despite the denial, the expert craftsman was then forced to draw the specifications from a picture of "The Chair" via a photo taken from the Library of Congress and while doing so inadvertently discovers at the Ford Theater **another identical and exact chair** just like the Abraham Lincoln assassination chair and from that identical chair builds a replica.

This now means at this time there are at least five identical chairs in circulation.

Is it any wonder then why the Henry Ford Museum did not want to show their perceived Abraham Lincoln assassination chair to the federal government or this expert furniture craftsman for fear that what they were holding may not be the original.

That said was the Henry Ford Museum then afraid that perhaps their prime exhibit was a fraud, a duplicate, a relic or Henry Ford got duped in his purchase back in 1929 and that perhaps what was being peddled just wasn't so, yet they apparently with guilty knowledge allowed the myth to continue in order to extract monies from unsuspecting visitors under false pretenses?

But more frightening then all of this is perhaps the museum was afraid that a scam whether deliberately designed or inadvertently designed would be exposed so they had to keep it hushed up!

50) In the article, "How Abraham Lincoln's assassination chair ended up in Michigan by Fritz Klug, the senior manager of creative programs at the Henry Ford Museum states, "It (the chair) was put into storage (at the Smithsonian Institute) in what turned out to be a hidden break area, we think for workers, because that's when the chair gets messed up. It appears people had access to it."

Now the chair was supposed to be in a secret secure spot, crated and stored without human access to it.

Obviously it was not!

Now, the Smithsonian Institute apparently had "The Chair" twice, once from 1869 to 1893 (24 years) and then from 1897 to 1928 (31 years) for a total of approximately 55 years. At the end of the second storage cycle Henry Ford purchased "a chair" or alleged "The Chair" for $2,400 dollars on the cheap.

So the Smithsonian Institute which alleges itself to be the largest and most distinguished museum in the world could not and did not protect this **National Treasure** from the destructive hands of men.

If "The Chair" at the time of Lincoln's assassination while being guarded had pieces stripped from it and deemed mutilated, so much so, the Assistant Secretary of War wanted those who were assigned to guard it imprisoned, what would happen to this same chair left unguarded, unprotected and neglected for 55 years when it was known to be important and monetarily valuable?

Therefore, I believe it is self-evident and stands to reason that the original "The Chair" during this time period had to be stolen, misplaced, or totally or partially destroyed without question.

This would make sense why the Henry Ford Museum's Lincoln's chair had little to no blood on it or why it was loaded with hair grease on the back inner side.

The reason being is the chair at the Henry Ford museum is not the original chair but a relic at best and a duplicate at worst.

51) An article published in the Detroit News, on April 6, 2015, named, "The Henry Ford to bring out chair Lincoln was shot in" by Jeff Karoub, Associated Press.

It stated this, "Museum officials say the chair (Lincoln's assassination chair) and car (John F. Kennedy limousine when he was fatally shot) are among the most visited artifacts in the museum, along with the bus Rosa Parks rode in when she refused to give up her seat to a white rider and help spark the civil rights movement."

Then the article states, "Many visitors wonder whether dark spots on the back of the (Lincoln) chair are Lincoln's blood. Not so, **say museum workers** : The stains are oil from other peoples hair who sat in the chair **before** that fateful night when Lincoln was shot by a pro-Confederacy actor, John Wilkes Booth."

First, I would like to emphasize that workers at the Henry Ford Museum made these comments according to the article!

Second, the museum workers stated that the Lincoln chair is among the most visited artifact. Which confirms the fact that the chair is a large tourist draw for monetary revenue.

Third, which I find extremely important is the fact based on what the Henry Ford Museum workers have stated is that human hair grease was on the chair **before** that fateful night in which Abraham Lincoln was shot.

So that means a chair with noticeable amount of human head grease on it was presented to the president of the United States to lean his 6'4" frame against it with his new suit.

Does that seem fitting for the president of the United States who is equal to the kings and queens of Europe to be given a chair imbedded with head grease containing possible head lice from who knows who's been sitting on it prior?

That doesn't make sense at all!

When I looked at the chair at the Henry Ford Museum in June 2015 the hair grease is readily apparent to the naked eye yet when I look at the photographs of the original chair taken approximately within 10 days after Abraham Lincoln's assassination, I see little to no head grease!

When I compared the present chair at the Henry Ford Museum and the original chair's picture taken from the United States Library of Congress within about 10 days after Abraham Lincoln's assassination <u>in the negative,</u> I see no grease in the original photo!

What does this mean?

It tells me "somebody is talking and they don't know what they are talking about" or, in fact they do know what their talking about.

I have to assume, therefore, that the Henry Ford Museum workers do know what they are talking about.

If this is so, I cannot accept the fact that the president of the United States was given a greasy spotted chair to watch a play on.

Fourth, the Henry Ford Museum workers stated that the chair had head grease <u>prior</u> to the assassination yet the Library of Congress photo taken just after the assassination shows no head grease.

Which would corroborate and agree with my diagnostic evaluation, which is, the president of the United States was given a very clean or near spotless chair for this fitting occasion.

My conclusion, to the quick is, that there are multiple identical Lincoln chairs in circulation.

Fifth, while at the Henry Ford Museum, in June 2015, with my daughter, Tracy, we sat in the Rosa Parks bus in the exact seat where we believe Mrs. Parks sat in and supposedly President Obama sat there also.

As we exited the bus I just happened to see a black lady there who was dressed in official garb who informed us she was a narrator for the bus, so I asked her this question, "How was this bus identified as the original bus, Rosa Parks sat in?"

She stated politely, "It was identified from the decal number (2857) on the front of the bus."

I replied, "Just the decal?"

She replied, "Yes!"

I couldn't believe it!

As I walked away, I looked at my daughter and stated, "Tracy, it looks like I just opened another can of worms and I am going to have to write another book!"

52) An article taken from the History Channel, dated September 21, 2012, titled "5 Things You May Not Know About Lincoln, Slavery and Emancipation" written by Sarah Pruitt.

This article in it's entirety seems to totally corroborate everything my father stated to me since 1990 or so that he witnessed on that critical day in question at Independence Hall with his friends.

To begin with in regards to slavery the article states, "Lincoln was no abolitionist," for "It (slavery) was sanctioned by the highest law in the land, the Constitution."

Then the article stated, "Abolitionist by contrast knew exactly what should be done about slavery. Slavery should be immediately abolished and freed slaves should be incorporated as equal members of society."

Third from the article it states, "Lincoln didn't believe that blacks should have the same rights as whites.

Though Lincoln argued that the founding father's phrase "All men are created equal" applied to blacks and whites alike, this did not mean he thought they should have the same social and political rights.

94

His views became clear during an 1858 series of debates with his opponent in the Illinois race for U.S. Senate, Stephen Douglas, who had accused him of supporting "negro equality."

In their fourth debate, at Charleston, Illinois, on September 18,1858, Lincoln made his position clear. "I will say then that I am not, nor ever have been, in favor of bringing about in any way the social and political equality of the white and black races," he began, going on to say that he **opposed** blacks having the right to vote, to serve on juries, to hold office and to intermarry with whites.

What he did believe was that, like all men, blacks had the right to improve their condition in society and to enjoy the fruits of their labor. In this way they were equal to white men, and for this reason slavery was inherently unjust."

Again this is basically the same content within the papers that my father read and stated as such.

Fourth, the article states, "Lincoln thought colonization could resolve the issue of slavery.

For much of his career, Lincoln believed that colonization—or the idea that a majority of the African-American population should leave the United States and settle in Africa or Central America—was the best way to confront the problem of slavery. His two great political heroes, Henry Clay and Thomas Jefferson, had both favored colonization; both were slave owners who took issue with aspects of slavery but saw no way that blacks and whites could live together peaceably.

Lincoln first publicly advocated for colonization in 1852, and in 1854 said that his first instinct would be "to free all the slaves, and send them to Liberia" (the African state founded by the American Colonization Society in 1821).

Nearly a decade later, even as he edited the draft of the preliminary Emancipation Proclamation in August of 1862, Lincoln hosted a delegation of freed slaves at the White House in the hopes of getting their support on a plan for colonization in Central America.

Given the "differences" between the two races and the hostile attitudes of whites towards blacks, Lincoln argued, it would be "better for us both, therefore, to be separated."

Lincoln's support of colonization provoked great anger among black leaders and abolitionists, who argued that African-Americans were as much natives of the country as whites, and thus deserved the same rights.

After he issued the preliminary Emancipation Proclamation, Lincoln never again publicly mentioned colonization, and a mention of it in an earlier draft was deleted by the time the final proclamation was issued in January 1863."

Again, this is precisely what my father alluded too when he read the Lincoln paper's contents witnessed with his friends at Independence Hall.

How could my father who was not a historian know so many precise details of the chair and the Lincoln papers if this event did not happen?

It can't be coincidence or random luck to remember so many vivid details of this witnessed event after almost 83 years or so.

Experience tells me when a person is so consistent in minor details without changing their story line to a witnessed event only adds to their credibility and is indicative of truthfulness.

Fifth, "Emancipation was a military policy", whose purpose was "to prevent the Southern rebellion from severing the Union permanently in two" and, "providing the Union with a new source of manpower to crush the rebellion."

This article basically states my father's comments which are in line with Lincoln's Emancipation Proclamation doctrine, free the slaves so they are not chattels of another as money or property then use them to fight the war unto victory.

When victory is finally achieved "unload this **black problem**" by deporting them elsewhere whether it be Liberia, England or Africa......**but in any case get rid of them, all of them**!

Again, that is exactly what my father stated over and over again throughout the years.

However, nobody knew then or now, as far as I know, what was to be "the final solution" to the "black problem" if Abraham Lincoln would have lived long enough to carry out his policy to fulfillment which would occur after the end of the Civil War.

Ultimately all blacks both free and slave were going to be deported, without just cause!

<u>In other words the black race was sold out and betrayed again!</u>

<u>Until divine intervention intervened and made it not happen!</u>

My father knew this around 1932 which led me to believe why his story must be told.

53) Lastly, the curator from Independence Hall also stated in her last message dated July 1, 2015 this, "Lincoln's view on slavery is well known. <u>Lincoln could be considered "racist" by today's standard in that he did not consider whites and blacks to be equal</u>."

Now that is precisely what my father was saying about the papers he read that were taken in regards to Abraham Lincoln's attitude towards blacks with his "final solution" upon the war ending.

So in my sincere opinion the Henry Ford Museum's claim that "The Chair" that they have had since 1929 is the original Lincoln assassination chair is in my assessment an almost certain impossibility which cannot be so when one considers the facts, probability, human nature, greed and circumstances.

Therefore, I am 75% certain or <u>beyond a reasonable doubt</u> that the chair at the Henry Ford Museum is "A Chair" and not "The Chair" and furthermore state that there is <u>no way</u> the Henry Ford Museum can prove the chair's originality in light of the chair's bizarre journey and undocumented and neglected history.

Now remember, the Henry Ford Museum has been stating that their chair is 100% original and not a replica, <u>yet they want us to accept it in good faith while denying us access to it to authenticate and prove its originality</u>.

Therefore, the burden of proof is not on me to disprove but rather on them, the Henry Ford Museum, to prove to the public in the public square that the chair that they have been peddling as 100 % original in all it's details is true!

I believe what I have presented in the public square are facts that any reasonable and prudent juror would agree to regarding the chair at the Henry Ford Museum which cannot be proven with 100% authenticity and therefore the American public are either being deliberately or inadvertently misled.

Case closed!

Chapter 8 - Conclusion

I believe the evidence speaks for itself, though nothing is 100% absolutely certain.

But then again it is not my job to prove "The Chairs" uncertainty 100%, but rather it is the Henry Fords Museum's responsibility to prove 100% "The Chairs" originality seeing that's what they have been peddling and claiming is legitimate while receiving money for the last 85 years.

I believe beyond a reasonable doubt based on the case facts available to me that my father seen the original Abraham Lincoln chair and original Abraham Lincoln papers at Independence Hall around 1932.

Further, I would also like to add this additional bit of information as told to me by my father after the book was published, in September 2015, that when I asked him, "Dad how many times did you see the original Abraham Lincoln chair at Independence Hall, Philadelphia, Pennsylvania?

To my surprise and with total confidence he replied, "Many times!"

So in closing Henry Ford, the auto industry magnate, bought "*A chair*" but not "*The Chair*" and played it off as original for economic gain at the near exact time his museum was opening.

"A Chair" now sits at the Henry Ford Museum at Greenfield Village for the last 85 years where it's chain of evidence is primarily based on a grainy film or a questionable unseen identification number in an attempt to pass it off to an unsuspecting public as original.

To those who may know more, I am all ears and I am from Missouri!

Show me?

That said, I think it is wrong if people take money ***knowingly*** under false pretences from the innocent for as my father said, "Who wants to see a replica and why would we take pieces of a chair and papers that was a replica?"

The big question is to those who peddle this chair as 100% original in it's entirety and if it is discovered it isn't so then, "Did they have guilty knowledge by knowing the chair was a fake in part or in whole while taking the public's money who trusted them that the chair was 100% original?

The American people are worth much more then that and transparency would be in order.

Furthermore, regarding the papers my father read, I would like to say this in closing, in my opinion, that the bringing of the black slaves to America, the horrific conditions of slavery that was endured, the Civil War, the Emancipation Proclamation to free these black people to fight for the Union in order to help win the war and turn the tide of battle.

Then the assassination of this good man Abraham Lincoln who appears to have had the intentions of deporting all the blacks back to Africa at the conclusion of the war has left me with the impression that it, the assassination, was an act of a higher power for the greater good for the black race.

They, the black race, are and were meant to be here whether they are liked as a race or not.

Therefore I accept "the handwriting on the wall" for I refuse to fight providence!

As a white man I say this to all white men for I know your pain and anger, despite that, the blacks are here for a reason and Lincoln was killed for a divine reason.

Think not?

A long time ago, the greatest being that ever walked the earth was sacrificed on a cross for humanity's sake.

Why not Lincoln for a race's sake?

If this is so, then whom am I to say differently if the black race is here despite my feelings one way or the other towards them.

This leads me back to the beginning of this book to what my wife, Denise, stated at the very moment I stared at the chair at the museum , "The chair is there, the blacks are here, Lincoln is dead. Who cares?"

My final answer, "God did and does!"

About the Author

News paperboy, bowling alley pinsetter, news paper jumper, bakers helper, toll collector, factory worker on" The Line", and, "The Pits".

Fireman and ambulance rescue driver.

Retired twenty-five year Lawman, assigned to" The Arab Corridor", Dearborn, Michigan.

State Certified Police S.W.A.T. Officer and Bomb Squad Supervisor seven years.

After winning a federal judgment by jury as a "whistleblower" against a tainted political "junta", along with a dispatched letter "that turned the heads of the Joint Chiefs of Staff, I was dined and requested "incognito" per a three letter agency to assist and initiate, an intelligent gathering network "via contacts through the Arab Corridor" from the United States to the Middle East.

Thirty-five years State of Michigan Licensed and Certified Public/ Private Polygraph Examiner with an A+ Rating Better Business Bureau. Expert Witness.

Eighteen years State of Michigan Licensed Private Investigator/Private Eye.

Military/Federal/Civilian trained Certified High Explosive Bomb Technician.

Trained in part with, C.I.A., F.B.I., A.T.F.,U.S. Navy U.D.T, Israeli's and New York Bomb Squad Technicians.

Licensed Aircraft Pilot. N.A.U.I Certified Scuba Diver.

Four time Marathon Runner, including Boston.

United States Marine Corps Captain with a prior Top Secret Clearance.

Brought under armed conditions the "Out of Country" votes and registrations of the newly developing and democratic nation of Iraq to concerned parties in Washington D.C.

Bachelor Degree in International Politics, University of Michigan.

Masters Degree(s) in Criminal Justice and Correctional Science, University of Detroit.

Traveled all of the Continental United States.

My books are true, written about adventure and exploration including conspiracies theories that I was directly involved in. My primary books are about real crime that I experienced first hand as a professional examiner/ interrogator in the streets and prisons of America.

www.ingramcontent.com/pod-product-compliance
Lightning Source LLC
Chambersburg PA
CBHW081634040426
42449CB00014B/3308